WHEN THE
GREAT CANOES CAME

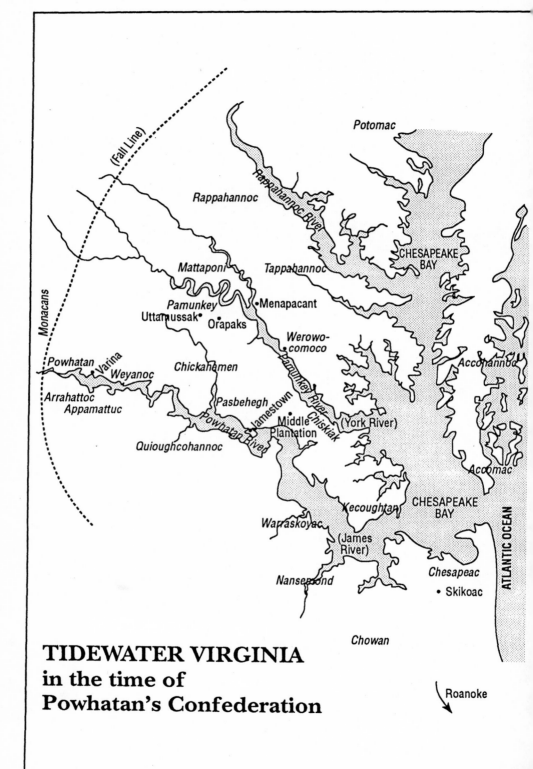

(Fall Line)

Monacans

Potomac

Rappahannoc

Rappahannoc River

CHESAPEAKE
BAY

Mattaponi

Tappahannoc

Pamunkey
Uttamussak•
Orapaks•

•Menapacant

Werowo-
comoco

Powhatan
Weyanoc

Varina

Chickahemen

Pamunkey River

Accohannoc

Arrahattoc
Appamattuc

Pasbehegh

Jamestown

Middle
Plantation

Chiskiak

(York River)

Powhatan River

Quioughcohannoc

Warraskoyac

Kecoughtan

CHESAPEAKE
BAY

(James
River)

Accomac

ATLANTIC OCEAN

Nansemond

Chesapeac
• Skikoac

Chowan

TIDEWATER VIRGINIA
in the time of
Powhatan's Confederation

Roanoke

Map by Michael Forsythe

WHEN THE GREAT CANOES CAME

BY MARY LOUISE CLIFFORD
ILLUSTRATED BY JOYCE HAYNES

A FIREBIRD PRESS BOOK

PELICAN PUBLISHING COMPANY
Gretna 1998

To Little Dove,
who devotes her life
to teaching about her people.

Library of Congress Cataloging-in-Publication Data

Clifford, Mary Louise.
    When the great canoes came / by Mary Louise Clifford ; illustrated
by Joyce Haynes.
        p. cm.
    Summary: A seventeenth-century Pamunkey Indian describes
how the coming of the English colonists has changed her life forever.
    ISBN 1-56554-646-6
    1. Powhatan Indians—Juvenile fiction. [1. Powhatan Indians—
Fiction. 2. Indians of North America—Virgina—Fiction.]
I. Haynes, Joyce, ill. II. Title.
PZ7.C62216Wh 1993
[Fic]—dc20

                                            92-27913
                                                 CIP
                                                  AC

Manufactured in the United States of America
Published by Pelican Publishing Company, Inc.
1000 Burmaster Street, Gretna, Louisiana 70053

Contents

POWHATAN FEDERATION CHIEFS (I-VIII) 1560-1686

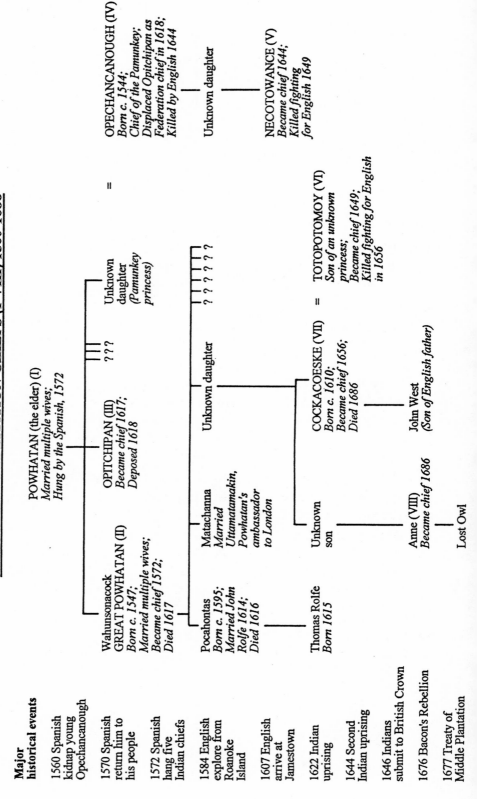

POWHATAN (the elder) (I)
Married multiple wives;
Hung by the Spanish, 1572

=

OPECHANCANOUGH (IV)
Born c. 1544;
Chief of the Pamunkey;
Displaced Opitchipan as
Federation chief in 1618;
Killed by English 1644

Unknown daughter

NECOTOWANCE (V)
Became chief 1644;
Killed fighting
for English 1649

Unknown daughter
(Pamunkey princess)

? ? ?

OPITCHIPAN (III)
Became chief 1617;
Deposed 1618

Wahunsonacock
GREAT POWHATAN (II)
Born c. 1547;
Married multiple wives;
Became chief 1572;
Died 1617

? ? ? ? ?

Unknown daughter

TOTOPOTOMOY (VI)
Son of an unknown
princess;
Became chief 1649;
Killed fighting for English
in 1656

=

COCKACOESKE (VII)
Born c. 1610;
Became chief 1656;
Died 1686

John West
(Son of English father)

Matachanna
Married
Utamatamakin,
Powhatan's
ambassador
to London

Pocahontas
Born c. 1595;
Married John
Rolfe 1614;
Died 1616

Unknown son

Anne (VIII)
Became chief 1686

Thomas Rolfe
Born 1615

Lost Owl

Major
historical events

1560 Spanish
kidnap young
Opechancanough

1570 Spanish
return him to
his people

1572 Spanish
hang five
Indian chiefs

1584 English
explore from
Roanoke
Island

1607 English
arrive at
Jamestown

1622 Indian
uprising

1644 Second
Indian uprising

1646 Indians
submit to British Crown

1676 Bacon's Rebellion

1677 Treaty of
Middle Plantation

CHAPTER ONE

The Loss
of Our Homeland

The most vivid memory of my childhood is of flight—a
hurried gathering of cooking pots and food and tools and
blankets and clothes into bundles, followed by a long trek
through the night.

The women had been preparing food around the evening
fires when the first of our braves came stumbling into our
village. We knew the minute they appeared that they had
not won the victory that Opechancanough had promised
them.

"We were betrayed! Armed settlers were waiting for us
all around Jamestown!"

"All of our braves that were posted anywhere close to the
island have been killed!"

Morsels of meat were passed to the warriors, as the
women absorbed the hurried accounts of the betrayal that
had turned the secret attack into a disaster. We children
listened raptly, and we knew better than to get underfoot
or pester the adults with our questions at such a moment.

A few more of our men straggled in as the bundles were
hastily wrapped in mats and tied for carrying. Wives and
children cried out when they heard that their husbands
and fathers had been struck down in the dawn attack.

In a surprisingly short time, we were ready for the trail.
The longhouses and gardens were simply abandoned as

each woman hoisted her bundle onto her back and distributed the smaller packages among her children. The canoes and a scout were left behind in case other braves might still make their way back to our village and find us gone. They would have no trouble tracing our path through the forest unless they were pressed from behind by enemies. All of our people know how to read the signs of who has passed by and where they have gone.

The sun had disappeared behind the trees when we set out, and I remember that the pace was very fast—much faster than our winter expeditions to the interior to hunt deer. The few braves who had returned followed at the rear with their weapons, ready to defend us if we were attacked.

At first, our swift passage through the shadowy forest seemed to be propelled by tension and drama, and I skipped along, buoyed by the excitement. But, as the hours wore past my usual sleeping time, the bundle I carried on my shoulder grew heavier and heavier. I began stumbling over tree roots, and my mother kept reaching out to steer me back onto the path.

I had long been convinced that I couldn't go any farther when the word to halt was passed down the line. Several of the women and older boys volunteered to keep watch while the men crawled into a thicket to sleep. I was curled up with my head resting on my bundle before my mother had a chance to unpack a fur blanket to throw over me.

The sun was overhead when I woke up. We were not allowed to make any noise or leave our hiding places to play. There was none of the festive atmosphere of a deer hunt, and the only relief to the forced idleness came late in the afternoon when six more of our braves caught up with us.

It was the season of rebirth—the willows along the streambeds were a shimmering pale green, the tips of ferns were showing in the mud, and the forest was streaked with dogwood and red bud—but we were too engrossed in our peril to notice the beauty around us. Without making any fires, we ate the cooked meat and *oppone* that the women carried wrapped in corn husks; then we set off again just before sunset.

Our route wound around the many marshes and in and out along the upper reaches of our river because we were seeking a refuge that would be too remote for the English to discover. We knew that the white men would be so angry at the deed attempted the previous morning* that, if they could find us, they would kill us all without mercy.

As I pause remembering the tension of the flight, the mat over the doorway of my longhouse is lifted and a lithe figure swings into the circle around the fire. It is Lost Owl. He touches his mother's shoulder to get her attention. Anne puts out a hand to restrain him, indicating with a nod that I am speaking and the boy must wait until I have finished. He rolls his eyes and sighs in disgust. Anne reaches for his hand and pulls him down onto the mat beside her. He does not come willingly.

I watch him screw up his dark cheeks to bare his perfect white teeth in protest. Anne lifts a finger to her mouth to silence him, and he turns his hostile black eyes in my direction. Anne picks up the thread of what I have said. "If the braves knew how angry the English would be, why did they attack them?"

I explain that the plan was to kill all the white invaders in the uprising, so there would be none left to retaliate.

"Did all of the braves believe that could happen?"

"There were those around the council fire who argued against it. They said that it would be impossible to keep the plan absolutely secret if all the many bands up and down the two rivers must cooperate to make it work."

"Were they not listened to in the tribal councils?"

Anne does not give up easily, and I reply that the dissenters spoke, but they were not as emphatic or as convincing in their arguments as Opechancanough.

Old Woman stirs and mutters, "The intrepid Opechan-

---

*Palm Sunday, 1622.

canough, chief of the Pamunkey." Her voice does not tell me whether she is expressing admiration or sarcasm.

I remind her that he was chief, not only of our Pamunkey tribe, but also chief of all the tribes that Powhatan had gathered into his alliance—including her own Weyanoc band.

"The supreme chieftain, consumed with hatred," she responds.

CHAPTER TWO

Exile

I start to tell Old Woman that there were good reasons for his hatred; but the frail figure lying on the sleeping platform by which we sit flutters her hands. "Don't defend him, Cockacoeske," she murmurs. "Go on with your story."

She is a plain-spoken woman, impatient with pretense and fancy words. I reach out and pat her gnarled and crippled hand, and nod in response to her protest. The pain that wracks her bent and twisted body tries her sorely. Knowing that she finds the sound of my voice soothing, and my memories a diversion from her suffering, relieves my anguish for her. She is the sister of the wife of one of my brothers. My brother married a princess in the Weyanoc band and went to live among her people on Powhatan's river. The Weyanoc were almost wiped out after the second uprising. One of our hunting parties rescued Old Woman as she wandered alone in the forest, confused and limping with pain. They brought her to my village because she had no kin left to turn to. With my brother and all of his family dead, there was no one to feed her or ease her suffering.

We thought she too would soon die, but the safety and serenity of my fireside renewed her strength and courage,

and she has clung to life with a tenacity that defies her creaking joints and twisted fingers. I am alone now too, and I take comfort in her feisty presence in my longhouse.

Aware of Lost Owl's brooding dark eyes challenging me, I debate whether to break off my story; but Old Woman mutters, "Go on."

We came finally, after three nights of fast marching, to a spot where our river was no more than a creek. The narrow glade beside it was well sheltered by a high, circular bank that must have been cut long ago by the floods of many springtimes. Downstream, a marsh prevented any approach to our hiding place from three sides.

The women built lean-tos of pine branches to shelter us if it rained, while the men set about constructing the framework for a large longhouse from young oak saplings driven into the ground. They tied the tops together into an arch with the inner lining of poplar bark that the women had stripped and pounded and twisted into cords. We had not carried enough rope to tie the mats that had wrapped our travel bundles in layers over the outside of the long-house. Much more rope and many more mats would be needed by the time each family built its own separate dwelling. Mats were also spread on the ground inside the longhouse, where we all slept. The many families were crowded side by side, with scarcely enough room to turn over in the night.

I remember that interlude as a happy time because we no longer had to be quiet and refrain from play. The half-grown boys were posted on scout duty on our one exposed flank, and the children romped along the water-side in noisy delight at being released from the forced silence of our long march. The stream flowed swiftly with the spring rain and was still icy cold, but so shallow that even the smallest of us was in no danger if we fell in. The new leaves on the trees were not yet dense enough to block the warmth of the sun, and the first small plants were poking through the thick blanket of dead leaves that covered the forest floor. Birds returning from the south chittered in the treetops, and we could hear frogs singing in the marsh downstream.

The longhouse was barely finished when the boys came running into camp to announce the arrival of Opechancanough and his bodyguard.

There was rejoicing because he and another dozen of our leaders had survived; but the atmosphere around the cooking fires that night was somber as we listened to the recounting of why the uprising had failed.

"Chanco had betrayed us," Anne interrupts with the answer.

Yes.

She has heard the story many times before, yet she is always patient and lets me tell it in my own way.

The plan had gone forward. Braves from the many tribes were scattered in all the English settlements, making themselves useful, and keeping the white men off guard. All would have gone as planned, had young Chanco not loved his English master and warned him in the night to be ready for the attack.

"How could he love his white master if the English were our enemies?" Lost Owl snaps. He glares at me with fierce eyes while he chews restlessly at a callous on his thumb.

"Richard Pace was very good to Chanco," I respond. "He adopted him, educated him, and treated him like his own son. Some of the English settlers were kind and wise and treated us like brothers. Our quarrel has always been with the governor and his council and his soldiers—they kept demanding our food stores and forcing us off our lands."

"But Chanco saved their lives too," Anne comments as I continue.

Chanco's warning was intended to save only his master's life; but Pace rowed immediately across the river to Jamestown to warn the governor, who sent out messengers as the dawn hour approached. Our braves within the circle reached by the warning were greeted with gunfire, and most of them were killed. Only in the outlying settlements did the attack go as planned.

Opechancanough was in a rage because all the bands on the peninsula—Kecoughtan, Weyanoc, Powhatan, Pamunkey, and Mattaponi—had to abandon their villages and flee to the interior, where the English could not follow. Yet he was not vanquished. That night, he stood behind the campfire in the longhouse, our people gathered around him, and swore that we would fight again another time. Even then, he was tall and gaunt and the oldest man I had ever seen. A man so old must be dear to powerful spirits. His skin hung in creased folds from his big bones, and the peak of his hair crest was nearly white. How he could speak—with eyes full of fire and a voice that shook the mats over our heads. He was not even one of us. His wife, whose royal blood had given him the privilege of being chief of the Pamunkey, was long dead. So convinced was he of the rightness of our cause that we believed him.

"You had to believe him, didn't you? He was your father," Anne murmurs.

"He was married to the sister of my true father, so I called him father—as we call all the husbands of the sisters of our mothers and fathers. Great Powhatan was my father because his half-sister was Opechancanough's wife, and she was my mother because she was my father's sister."

Old Woman, buried in a pile of rabbit skins, chuckles. She remembers how confusing the English found this— they were never quite sure who we all were. "They know who you are, Cockacoeske. They call you Queen of the Pamunkey. Doesn't that make you proud?"

I smile in response, but ignore her question because of the disturbing presence of Lost Owl. Explaining to him what the English do is difficult because they are really beyond my understanding. They tried to give Great Powhatan a crown when he was already chief of all our people. What does it change when foreigners call you king?

CHAPTER THREE

The First Reprieve

"Do the English make you proud?" Lost Owl glares at me, and it takes effort to meet the contempt in his eyes without flinching.

"We can discuss that, if you like," I murmur finally.

"Do they?"

I wish I could give more convincing answers to the boy's questions. How does one explain kings and queens and armies, or make sense of the English rules of government when they are so different from our own? I have been chief of my tribe for most of Lost Owl's mother's lifetime— thirty *c'hunks* now—thirty migrations of the geese that fly out of the north as the leaves are falling, calling *c'hunk* to each other. I still wonder if our lives might be better if we had followed some other course.

I choose my words carefully; then I explain.

So many of our people were killed in the fury unleashed by the two uprisings under Opechancanough's command that those of us who survived finally decided that we had no other recourse than to make our peace with the English and try to live in harmony with them as Powhatan had done so many years before. We talked of fleeing, but there was really no place to go. Our enemies, the Monocans, controlled all of the land in the hills to the west and were constantly raiding the fringes of tidewater. The Susquehannoc threatened from the far north. The tribes along the seacoast in the east and to the south spoke our language and were our friends, but we could only move onto their lands if we became their subjects. Besides, they were having their own difficulties with the white men coming in from the eastern sea in their great canoes pushed by the wind to establish settlements along their shores.

When the second uprising failed, and Opechancanough was killed at Jamestown, the time finally came when the younger men could prevail and sue for peace.*

Even then, good relations were not quickly restored. Too much bitterness and hatred had accumulated for the English to easily accept our submission. Our braves had to fight beside the white men against Monocan attacks from the interior before we were trusted again.

Anne nods her dark head wisely as she anticipates my words. "That's how my father and your husband Totopotomoy were killed," she says.

"That is true."

Anne never saw her father, who was my older brother, because she was born right after the last uprising. My own tall, strong brave might still be chief had he not also fallen while fighting for the English. Had he lived, I might never have had to assume his title.

Anne sees the sadness that comes with my memories of him, but she misinterprets it. "Would you have preferred not to be chief, Cockacoeske?"

It is not a question I can answer, because I had no choice. I explain to her that the treaty that Necotowance signed with the English after the second uprising let us move back to the land on the Pamunkey river that we considered to be our own.** It was much closer to Orapaks—

---

*1644.
**1646.

our home before the uprising—than the refuge in which
we hid for the many *c'hunks* between the uprisings. That
put us within two days' march of Jamestown. Someone
had to take charge and deal with the English if we were
going to be their neighbors. After Totopotomoy's death,
the men shrank from assuming that responsibility.

"Couldn't you have stayed in your hiding place?" Lost
Owl asks.

I tell him no, out how can a boy who didn't experience
that exile understand the privation of the twenty *c'hunks*
we spent there?

"Consider, Lost Owl, that our people have always lived
on the great bay that the English named after the Chesapeac
tribe and on the broad waters that flow into it. We depended
on the waters for much of our food and to carry our
canoes. Over the years, we had found the most fertile soil
along the banks and we cleared broad fields for our
gardens of corn, beans, melons, and pumpkins."

I explain that the forests and marshes of the interior
were far less hospitable. Not only were they far from the
rivers and the bay, but they were also too close to the fall
line in the rivers—where the streams of the interior hills
drop into the flat country of the daily tides. The hill
country belonged to our ancient enemies, and we were
always in danger of them discovering us during their
hunting forays. Our numbers were too small to prevail if
they decided to drive us out.

"So the chiefs gave in," Lost Owl mutters.

"They had to," I countered. "We knew that we could
never thrive in that hostile environment. Before the second uprising, Necotowance and Totopotomoy had already
laid the groundwork to let us escape it."

"How?"

They saw their opportunity when Thomas Rolfe, the son
of Pocahontas and the Englishman John Rolfe, came under
safe conduct to our hiding place shortly before the second

uprising.* He was in his early manhood then, and had only recently returned to the land of his birth after growing up in England. His baby nurse, Matachanna, was still living. His pilgrimage to the interior was spurred by his desire to finally meet his mother's people, of whom he had no remembrance because he was only a baby when Pocahontas died and his father left him in England with an uncle.

Opechancanough, who always considered Pocahontas to be a traitor, received her son coldly and barely tolerated his presence. Necotowance and Totopotomoy, however, made a special effort to win his confidence. They knew that Opechancanough would not live much longer. When he was gone and the younger men took over, they wanted Thomas Rolfe to intercede with the English governor in Jamestown, so that negotiations could begin to restore the friendship that had existed during the Peace of Pocahontas.

Anne looks at me with a puzzled frown and serious brown eyes. "And yet there was another attack on the white men after Thomas Rolfe left? Why did Necotowance and Totopotomoy let that happen?"

In response to her question, I can only sigh. One would have to have lived with Opechancanough to understand why none of us had the courage to tell that formidable old man to step aside and stop pursuing his hopeless revenge.

By then, Opechancanough had counted almost a hundred *c'hunks*. He was so infirm that he ordered the younger men to carry him into battle—but imagine what power the spirits had bestowed on him to permit him to live so long. He never let us forget that he was the chief of Powhatan's federation. He stood at Powhatan's right hand through all the years in which he was bringing the bands together. Powhatan designated Opitchipan to succeed to his title, but when Opechancanough challenged him in the tribal

---

* 1641 or 1642.

council, the braves supported him. He ruled with an iron will ever after.

The braves of my generation never had the confidence of our earlier leaders. We were refugees—our land, our past, and our traditions were destroyed. Both Orapaks and Uttamussak, where stood the most sacred temples of our priests, were burned to the ground. The core of our lives had been taken from us. Only Opechancanough seemed to have an absolute conviction of the course we should follow. The younger men deferred to him because of his great experience and age. The time finally came when his obsession was beyond reason, but no one had the courage to tell him that we would no longer follow him.

"How sad." The voice, barely a whisper, is Old Woman's. Yes, it was sad. Although our warriors succeeded in killing more of the white settlers in the second uprising than twenty *c'hunks* earlier in the first, the white men were far more numerous then. We were defeated again, and left as helpless as scattered driftwood washed up after a storm.

How different it was from the days of my childhood. When Great Powhatan held the allegiance of every band from the capes at the entrance of the bay to the fall line on the three rivers, the whole land was ours. In that time, the council fire was surrounded by chiefs, and the warriors under Powhatan's command numbered in the thousands. In my reign, I have been lucky to muster a hundred able men bearing arms. One does not exercise one's authority with great confidence when dealing from a position of weakness.

Anne reaches for my hand and gently rubs its ridges of veins and tendons in an effort to console me. "The English have respected you, Cockacoeske. You have signed a treaty with them, and their king in London has sent you royal robes and a silver medallion to wear around your neck."

How she loves those trinkets—the glint of the silver and

the rich colors of the woven fabrics. I do not need to remind her that Necotowance's treaty ended our freedom by making us subjects of the English Crown. I comment only that gifts from London have never spurred the governor at Jamestown to protect us from our enemies.

She is quick in her reply. "Nor did he protect his own settlers. Nathaniel Bacon could not have rebelled if he had."

That is true, but we were caught in the middle. Nathaniel Bacon could not distinguish a Monocan from a Pamunkey. If we had red skin, we were his enemies, and our people were killed in spite of my treaty with the English. I was helpless to prevent it.

CHAPTER FOUR

Another Attack

"May I speak to my mother now?" Lost Owl snaps.

I nod my permission.

Anne rises and follows the boy out, and I am left musing about this rebellious youngster, son of the princess who will soon succeed me. Every night, I search my dreams for some clue to this boy's future. Will Lost Owl ever be willing—or able—to assume my mantle?

Because I am so accustomed to his anger, he surprises me the next day by following his mother into my longhouse when she comes for her usual visit.

I raise my eyebrows at his greeting.

"Mother has been telling me what Nathaniel Bacon and his rebellion did to us. My father can no longer hunt or join war parties because of the injuries he received in an attack that Bacon led against the English governor."

I nod. By rights, Anne's husband should become chief. She is a princess, the channel for royalty in our line; but he is crippled now, and there are no other males in his generation with the right ancestry and enough conviction and faith in the future to assume the mantle of leadership.

"That's why my mother will succeed you," the boy continues.

I nod again. Anne senses the presence of our ancestors; she feels them walking by our sides.

Anne sits down on the mat and pulls her son down beside her. She tells him, "I was with Cockacoeske when the messenger from the chief of the Appamattucs came to our village with the news that young Bacon was rallying the outlying settlers to take up arms against Governor Berkeley. The governor had failed to protect them against the Monocan raiders sweeping down out of the hills. We were still clustered around the Appamattuc brave, hanging on his words, when a horseman from Jamestown rode in with a summons for Cockacoeske to appear before the council."

Lost Owl turns his demanding eyes on me. "Did you know what they wanted?"

"No, but I chose my costume very carefully, to remind the English that I am a *weroansqua*.* Over my shoulders, I draped my best deerskin mantle, which falls from my neck to my feet and is trimmed along the edges with deep, twisted fringe. On my head, I placed the high crown of *peake* that I reserve for ceremonial occasions—the one that is woven of black and white *wampum* as wide as a man's hand. Although I understand the language of the English very well, I took my son John West, whose father was an English colonel, and Cornelius Dabney, the Englishman who interprets for me, with me to emphasize my sovereignty."

"You trusted an Englishman to interpret for you?" Lost Owl eyes me with disgust.

"All the white men are not evil. Cornelius Dabney and a few others have always tried to treat our people fairly. He presents my arguments clearly in my negotiations with the English governor. A wise chief must know who to trust."

Lost Owl glares his skepticism but says nothing.

---

*The English term "squaw" comes from the Algonkin title *weroansqua*—the feminine of *weroance,* which means "chief."

When we arrived at the State House in Jamestown, there was much confusion in the yard. Clusters of soldiers were standing or sitting about and others were rushing here and there, as the guards ushered us ceremoniously through the big wooden doors. I had just seated myself at the council table and the committee members resumed their seats, when they expressed their alarm over the fighting on the frontier and asked me how many braves I could provide to assist in their defense.

The question dumbfounded me. "Do you not remember that it was in just such circumstances as these that my husband Totopotomoy and ninety of his men lost their lives twenty *c'hunks* ago?" I demanded of them. "The bulk of our fighting force—and what compensation have my people received for that loss? Nothing!"

As Cornelius Dabney was translating my protest, the memory of my tall, strong brave swept over me—along with the shadow of a dream that has come to me so many times since. In this nightmare I see his lifeless body abandoned among his comrades beside a distant forest trail. The vultures are feasting, and I mourn because no grave receives him, no loving hands retrieve his weapons, no cairn of stone marks his final resting place, and the sleeping remains of the chiefs at Orapaks do not mark his passing.

My personal grief could hardly be explained to the English, but I spoke at length, arguing that the loss of our chief and so many of our able men in those earlier battles had weakened our band. I bemoaned how few there were left to take up arms.

The English countered with a promise that our men would be provided with English weapons and taught how to use them. That was a very tempting proposition because my men wanted guns above all else. The council members asked me again how many warriors my village could supply. We talked back and forth for some time, until I realized that this was the central topic of this meeting— the only reason I had been summoned. My protests were of little concern to them.

In my mind, I counted my fighting men and realized that twelve was the most that could be spared from our little cluster of longhouses. A few of the men must stay in the village to protect our women and children. The council was disappointed with such a small number and urged me to make more of our braves available, but I stood firm. Cornelius Dabney reminded them again how thin our ranks were, and they finally accepted his argument. They all thanked me profusely for coming, and Cornelius Dabney assured me in parting that the tie between the English and my people had been strengthened.

In the following days, we learned that Bacon had appeared with a hundred armed men at Jamestown and had demanded a commission from Governor Berkeley authorizing him to wipe out the tribes that had killed over five hundred settlers on the frontier. The assembly gave Bacon the authority he wanted.

The next moon had barely been sighted when a swarm of Bacon's men came riding down on our village, armed and with no hint of friendship in their headlong approach.* They shot at the first of my people they encountered, and my men were running for their own weapons when I stopped them.

"I have given the English my promise of friendship," I shouted. "We will not fight these marauders! We must flee instead!"

"I remember that!" Lost Owl interrupts. "The shouting— and everyone running."

"You were barely a toddler," Anne protests. "I had to carry you."

"I remember," he repeats doggedly. "It was the first time I was ever afraid."

Anne looks at me. "Maybe he does remember."

It is possible. We were all afraid.

---

* 1676.

We abandoned everything—longhouses, food stores, clothing, tools—except what few valuables we could snatch up in our hands as we rushed into the forest. Fortunately, it had recently rained very hard, and the land was steaming in the heat and dampness of summer. The ground was soggy, making poor footing for horses. The attackers were mired briefly in the swampy hollow beside the village. Old Woman was carried speedily off on the back of a sturdy youth. We all got away, except for two who moved too slowly—one small child and my elderly nurse—whom Bacon's men carried off.

I learned later that they ordered that sweet lady to lead them to our hiding place. She deliberately took them in the opposite direction. When they discovered her deception, they smashed her skull with a musket butt, mutilated her body, and abandoned it in the forest. She had a dear heart and gentle hands that soothed my woes ever since I was born. We never found the child.

Even then, those marauders did not give up. They kept searching until they found our temporary camp, and they attacked us again. Some of us escaped a second time, but Bacon's men captured forty-five of our people and carried away all of the small treasures that we had managed to carry with us in the flight from our village—mats, baskets of *wampum peake,* pieces of English cloth, everything we owned.

Those of us who escaped trekked in the midsummer heat far into the wilderness, back to the area in which we hid during those long years of exile. We huddled there, without any bear grease to repel the flies and mosquitos, as chains of thunderstorms shook the earth. Small game and birds were all we had to eat, and we had no extra clothes at all.

Mine was the responsibility to devise a plan for avoiding another long sojourn far from our homeland. I consulted with the priests, who studied their sacred circles of sticks and grain to see what the future held. We burned what little tobacco we could find, wafting the smoke through our tiny camp to purify the air. The priests decided finally that

I should return alone to our village and throw myself on the mercy of the English. Surely they would not kill me, whom they called Queen of the Pamunkey. They would have to listen when I told them of our treaty with the governor and of our guides who were marching with the colonial militia—Anne's husband among them.

My people were reluctant to let me go, but I saw no other way, so I set out. It was a long trek with no clear path to follow at first, and I trudged through the sodden forests with many detours around the marshes and feeder streams. I found that I tired much earlier than in my younger years, and I felt suffocated by the hot, sticky haze that blanketed the landscape.

When finally I reached the well-trodden trail that led to our village, I felt relieved that my ordeal was almost over. Then a terrible stench made my stomach heave as I stumbled over the bloody and bloated body of my slain nurse. The sight of her smashed skull was so sickening that I turned blindly aside and went streaking through the forest, propelled by the horror of what they had done to that beloved old lady.

When I regained my senses, I was completely lost.

Anne is remembering too. She strokes her son's bare arm with one finger and shakes her head. "You were gone for fourteen days," she reminds me, "and had nothing to eat but the blackberries that you found in the forest."

I nod ruefully. "It took me all that time to come to my senses."

When I finally found the hiding place, I was so weak that I could barely walk. I could hardly swallow the rabbit stew that I was given.

Even the relief of being reunited with my people couldn't assuage the misery of being forced from our homes again. I worried through the steaming summer nights when not a breath of air stirred the leaves in the forest. What path should we be following?

Finally, I sent a runner—a sturdy boy who was willing

and daring, but not yet old enough to be a warrior—to find our braves who were marching with the English troops.

While he was gone, we got word that Governor Berkeley had fled to the eastern shore of the bay, relinquishing control of the entire peninsula to Bacon, with his head-quarters at Middle Plantation, just inland from Jamestown.*

When my runner returned, he was accompanied by my son John West and eight survivors of the twelve I had sent to serve the governor. Among them was Anne's husband, an arm around a companion's shoulder, hopping along on one leg because his thigh had been shattered by a stray musket shot. He told us that we should stay hidden until it was clear who would win this contest between the English governor and Bacon's rebellious troops.

---

* Later renamed Williamsburg.

CHAPTER FIVE

Back in Favor

"Go on."

The harsh voice snaps me out of the reverie I have drifted into. I lift my head to meet Lost Owl's fierce eyes. "I have a right to know these things," he snaps. "You've no right to keep them from me."

"I never intended to keep them from you," I protest. "I didn't realize that you were interested.

He sniffs. "What happened to Nathaniel Bacon?"

I am so startled by his accusation that I must take a deep breath before I can speak.

The leaves were falling in swirls of red and gold, and the children had been sent to gather nuts in the forest when we learned that Nathaniel Bacon had suddenly fallen ill and died. The news brought the faint hope of a reprieve for us, but we waited in our hiding place far upstream until we were sure that Governor Berkeley had returned to Jamestown. Then we moved cautiously back down to the village from which Bacon's men had driven us, and set about rebuilding our lives.

The trees were bare and the edges of the streams were crusted with ice before we were certain that the rebellion had collapsed completely and the Crown was again in full control of the colony. We sent a petition to the House of

Burgesses, requesting the restoration of the possessions and land that had been stolen or abandoned when Bacon's men attacked us.

The elected representatives in the assembly, many of them from the rural areas that had suffered from Monocan attacks, paid little attention to our claim. They agreed to give back only those items that we could prove were ours, and they demanded that we return any horses or goods in our possession that belonged to the English.

Old Woman snorts and waves her misshapen hands. "What a ridiculous order! We had been robbed of everything we owned."

She speaks the truth.

There were not enough able-bodied men in the band during our weeks in hiding—nor were they armed to conduct a proper deer hunt—so we had few skins to make into clothes or blankets. All of our *wampum peake* was gone, leaving us nothing to trade with other bands. No seed corn or dried beans were left for the spring planting. We managed to grow a crop of gourds to fashion into water containers. We had made mats and baskets from the marsh grasses while we were in exile, and cured rabbit, squirrel, and raccoon pelts; but that was the extent of our worldly goods as we set about reconstructing the longhouses that Bacon's men had torched.

Imagine our surprise two moons later at being invited to the new guardhouse at Middle Plantation to discuss another treaty of friendship with the English. We knew that Bacon and his men had burned Jamestown, but we had not yet seen the new settlement that the English were raising on slightly higher ground in the center of the peninsula.

The invitation came from a group of men, newly arrived from England in one of the great canoes pushed by the wind, who called themselves the king's special commissioners. They said that King Charles had instructed them to renew the colonial government's peace agreement with the people who were their neighbors. They reminded the assembly that we provided the best guards along the frontier, because we alone stood between the colony and the hostile tribes of the interior.

Accordingly, on the day that was King Charles II's birthday, I took my son John West with me to Middle Plantation to meet with these special commissioners.* The governor and his council were all there, dressed in ceremonial robes and seated in a fine new chamber that smelled of fresh wood. I was joined by the surviving chiefs of Weyanoc, Nottoway, Nansemond, and Appamattucs. After the meeting was called to order, the treaty was read to us by the chairman. My interpreter, Cornelius Dabney, explained each of the twenty-one articles to us in our own language and assured us that the English now regarded our tribes as reunited under my authority—as they had been in Powhatan's time. Because I trusted him, and because our people were weary of fighting, I wanted to believe his promises.

Lost Owl snorts, and I cannot argue with him that past experience gave us every reason to be wary of such promises. Cornelius Dabney was obviously sincere, but he had no authority with which to protect us.

He escorted me within the bar of the court to sign this Treaty of Middle Plantation on behalf of my people and the other tribes. The governor asked the queen of Weyanoc, the king of Nottoway, and the king of Nansemond to also sign. The king of Appamattucs was ignored because the English had accused some of his people of murder.

Each of us knelt in turn and kissed the parchment to publicly acknowledge that we held our titles and lands as tributaries of the great king of England. To conclude the ceremony, the ranks of English soldiers outside were ordered to attention and set off their usual blasts of musket fire and small shot and fireworks.

---

*May 29, 1677.

Anne tips her head from side to side wistfully. She prefers to be called by the public English name we gave her, rather than by her private name in our own language. She loves the stately pomp and color of the English ceremonies. "How I wish I could have been there," she says.

"It was very staid," I assure her. "Much more staid than the festivities three *c'hunks* later when the new governor, Thomas Culpeper, arrived from England. He brought gifts from the king to the chiefs who had signed the Treaty of Middle Plantation."

Anne wraps her arms around her knees and rocks back and forth in delight at the memory. "I shall never forget that. The troops lined up in their metal breastplates and helmets, with pennants on their lances. The governor, dressed all in scarlet and white, made his speech of appreciation on behalf of the king. They gave you a silver and gold brocade gown lined with cherry-colored silk—so smooth that it felt like flower petals—and a scarlet robe with a purple manto lining to wear over it and for your head, a cap of crimson velvet, trimmed with white ermine fur. When they hung the silver necklace with King Charles' badge around your neck, I could have wept because you were so beautiful—as splendidly gowned and jeweled as the governor's lady."

Lost Owl squats beside her with a small frown between his straight black brows, studying the rapture on her face.

I smile too over my own recollection of the deference with which I was treated. I cannot pretend that those symbols of recognition and authority did not bring me a brief moment of exultation.

"They dressed John West in a scarlet suit," Anne rambles on, "with scarlet stockings embroidered with black silk. They put a white beaver hat trimmed with a gold and silver band on his head and gave him pistols decorated with gold and silver and a finely embroidered belt to hold his new sword. He was as elegant as any of the Englishmen present, and he looked every inch a prince."

"We were honored by those expressions of appreciation," I concede, glancing again at Lost Owl's sour expression, "but brocade robes and fur hats have not put food in our bellies nor restored any of our ancestral rights to us. The English carry on their endless discussions of who our land belongs to, but they seem incapable of understanding when we tell them that the Creator Ahone gave the land to all our people at the beginning of time. No one person can own it. We have only the right to use it." I cannot suppress a sigh. "The English dress me like a queen but refuse to recognize that all of the lands between our rivers—where hundreds of settlers have now spread their tobacco plantations—are rightfully ours to use."

Lost Owl turns his scowl toward me. The childlike delight fades from Anne's face, and she peers at me with the weary eyes of middle age. Finally, she makes a flat statement.

"Opechancanough understood that from the beginning, didn't he? If Powhatan had listened to him, these lands would still be ours."

CHAPTER SIX

Consider, Lost Owl

Unlike the English, who string time out in a series of numbered years, our people remember our past in association with important events. I always connect Anne's birth with Opechancanough's death—his passing marked the beginning of our attempt to restore friendship with the English, which soon ended our exile. Anne's lifespan corresponds exactly with the period during which we have acknowledged ourselves as tributaries of the English Crown.

Our people respect Anne for her good practical sense as well as for the dignity that she bestows on her role as wife and mother. Her son Lost Owl is of the age where he should be passing through his initiation rites, but there are not enough priests left to lead a *huskenaw*. When Anne joins me on the mat the next afternoon, he has followed her and stands awkwardly to one side, rubbing one foot over the other ankle and twisting his thumbs together. I wait for him to speak.

"Yesterday you were telling us about the rebel Bacon and the Treaty of Middle Plantation."

"Yes, son."

"My mother says that you often tell stories to help Old Woman pass the time and sometimes you tell the lore that

37

you learned around the campfires in Great Powhatan's time."

"That is true."

"She says that if we had lived in your time, the boys my age would have all gone into the forest with the priests and stayed there for months being tested in courage and endurance and learning all the laws and history of our people."

I nod. "And you would have returned to us as men, with new names that indicated how you had responded to your testing and with the skills needed to become respected braves."

Lost Owl hunches his shoulders. "It's not fair that we no longer do the *huskenaw.*"

"There is little in our lives today that is fair, son."

The boy stops wringing his hands and scowls at me. He is at an age when he hates to accept the wisdom of his elders.

"If we can't do the *huskenaw,* at least you could tell us the tribal lore," he mutters.

I catch my breath. "I had no idea that you were willing to listen."

He tosses his head without looking at me. "Some of us wouldn't mind."

"Bring them."

"You will have to start at the beginning so we can understand." His voice is grudging and he peers at me out of the corner of his eye.

"Do you mind?" I ask Old Woman.

"Of course not. Bring your friends, son."

"But will Cockacoeske answer all of our questions?" he asks her rather than me.

Old Woman lifts her shoulders. "Try asking her."

The boy glances defensively at me.

"Knowing that you are interested would give me great pleasure," I assure him.

Lost Owl collects the two striplings who are his constant companions, Savage Bear and Shad Running, and they settle on the mat beside Anne. "Start at the very beginning," Lost Owl commands me.

My heart quivers as I note the guarded expressions that the youngsters turn to me. How sad it is that there is no one among us trained to pass on the traditions of our tribe as the priests did in my childhood. They are all gone now. Those orators who entranced us around the evening fires on those crisp winter nights of long ago were either killed in battle or struck down by the plagues that the white men brought with them. No one is left to tie us to the past or guide us into the future, except the few of us who remember the heroic epics from having heard them so many times when we were children. We are growing old and forgetful, weary from our long struggle to survive. Who among us has the energy—or the faith in the future—to tell those ancient stories to our children so the spirits of our ancestors will truly walk among them? There is so much that should be recorded in my people's memories before I pass beyond the sunset; but who among the young will believe in this time of trouble that deeds of long ago might sustain them now?

I collect my thoughts because my words must erase the boys' skepticism, or the effort will be wasted.

In the beginning, and for all time, was the Creator Ahone, who gave us the land and the sea, the sun and the moon, the birds and the beasts, the cold and the warmth. When he had arranged all of these things, he gave to each of his people an immediate spirit of their own to dwell with them and protect them from evil and disaster. The spirit he gave to us was Okee, whose image we enshrined in our temples, and whose wisdom our priests invoked when danger threatened us. He has been our guardian since time began.

Lost Owl flexes his shoulders and peers up from under fierce, dark eyebrows.

Okee's principle temple was at Orapaks, where I was born. In the temple, all the important ceremonies to bless the planting and give thanks for the harvest took place. Our chiefs were laid to rest on the platform behind Okee's statue, and our priests kept watch day and night over the sacred fire that burned below his image.

"The English burned Orapaks to the ground," Lost Owl interrupts.

"Yes, but that comes much later in the story," I chide him gently.

The land that Ahone gave us was good. The forests spread their sheltering crowns over our heads and were full of nut and fruit trees that gave us food. Wild game ran in abundance before our hunters. The many rivers and the bay teemed with fish and oysters and crabs, which we learned to catch. We made dugouts from tree trunks to travel over the water. Our neighbors to the north—the Rappahannoc and Potomac—spoke our language and were friendly. We also understood and traded with the Chowan to the south.

To the west, the Monocans spoke in words we did not understand and followed a different spirit, but they were far enough away that we only encountered them during the lean winter months when we trekked inland toward the hills in search of deer. On the peninsula between Powhatan's river and our Pamunkey river, the many bands who lived along the shores were related to each other, spoke the same tongue, and cooperated in seeking the common good. You youngsters have never seen most of this country between the bay and the fall line because the English no longer permit us access to our ancestral lands.

"They have even renamed our rivers," Savage Bear comments. "They call Powhatan's river the James, after their own king, and our Pamunkey river is the York to them."

"Be patient. That too comes much later in the story."

The English at Jamestown Island were not the first white men to come up Powhatan's river in their great canoes pushed by the wind. The Spanish came into the bay much earlier, and our people were terrified because they had never seen canoes propelled by sails before, nor men with white skins.*

They thought that these strangers must be spirits because the souls of our own departed dead, when they pass through the path of the setting sun, are cleansed until they are white.

The Spanish encountered the young son of one of the Chickahamen chiefs, paddling alone in his canoe on the river. They took him on board their great canoe and sailed out between the capes into the eastern ocean and disappeared. His people despaired because there was no way to rescue him; they mourned his loss and never expected to see him again.

Lost Owl is familiar with some of this and interrupts me. "But he came back—all dressed in Spanish clothes—and no one recognized him!"

"How do you know that?" Shad Running challenges him.

"Because he was Opechancanough, who eventually became chief of our tribe."

"Is that true?" Dark eyes turn to me.

"It was Opechancanough."

"It must have been a very long time ago."

I do some calculations to measure the time. "Opechancanough always said that he had seen fourteen migrations of the geese before he was kidnapped. He lived through a hundred migrations before he was killed, and his death

---

*1560.

was over forty *c'hunks* ago." The boys' eyes grow round as
they try to project themselves that far back in time.

"How did he escape from the Spanish?" Lost Owl wants
to hear the details again.

I think back to my own childhood and the many times I
listened enthralled as Opechancanough told us that amaz-
ing tale.

They took him far away from his homeland—all the way
to countries they called Cuba and Mexico and Spain. He
knew that he could never find his way home alone—even if
he could escape. He was clever, young as he was, and he
decided that he would do whatever was necessary to win
his captors' confidence in the hope that he could discover
some way to prompt them to return to his river.

The Spanish seemed to be particularly intent on convincing him to forsake Okee and worship their god. The
boy realized that they earned some sort of special status
with their god by bringing non-believers into the fold. He
agreed to become a Christian, and he told anyone who
would listen that he would convince all of his people to do
the same if he was taken home. Eventually, he met some
Spanish priests called Jesuits. They believed him, and
they petitioned their king for permission to return to our
country and convert our people.

On the first trip, when they sailed from Cuba, they
didn't go far enough north to find our bay, and he was
heartbroken when they turned back. Finally, they set out
again.* This time, they found the capes into our bay and
sailed up Powhatan's river until Opechancanough recognized the inlets and marshes that he had been taken from
ten *c'hunks* earlier.

He was absolutely ecstatic. He had them anchor and go
ashore in a forested area where he knew there were no
villages or tilled fields. Their progress up the river had
been watched from the shore, of course, and some of his

---

*1570.

own people were waiting on the beach when the Spaniards landed their longboat. Opechancanough's brothers were very wary of the huge canoe swinging against its anchor, the strange clothes, and the pale skin of the foreigners whom they still couldn't believe were living people.

They soon noted, however, that one in the group who disembarked had skin as dark as theirs. Although he was dressed like the others and wore his hair long on his shoulders, he spoke to them in their own language. They were astounded and could hardly believe that this was the long-lost Opechancanough. They ran their hands over his green jacket and his cotton britches and admired the boots that came up to his knees. They laughed at the strange hat he wore and chided him for his ridiculous hairstyle. They said that no brave could draw bow with his hair hanging over his right shoulder like that.

He laughed too and told them that he would have his hair cut properly as soon as he returned to his village. First, he had to get rid of the five Jesuits who had come on the ship with him. His brothers wondered what kind of magic he would use, but he had a scheme in mind.

He had deliberately chosen a landfall where the forest was suitable only for hunting grounds. The Spaniards expected to find gardens and cornfields and a bountiful food supply, but he told them they had arrived during a disastrous drought which had made it impossible to grow any crops. Consequently, the people who ordinarily lived there had moved into the interior to seek wild game. Because there was no food to be had in that area, the Jesuits should return to Florida.

"Will they believe that?" his brothers asked. "The season has been dry, but there are plenty of wild game and fowl in the forest. The women and children are gathering hickories and walnuts even now."

"The Spaniards don't know that," he said. "We must be careful to keep them away from our fields and villages."

"Do you really think they will leave without exploring?" the brothers asked.

"They do not have time to explore; the food on the ship is running low. The voyage from Florida has taken much longer than they expected, and the ship's crew has already eaten a portion of the supplies that were put on board for the priests. The Spaniards must either find food immediately or hurry home," Opechancanough explained.

"Won't they take you with them if they go?" they asked.

"They will try, but they will not succeed this time. They have no soldiers with them to frighten my people because I made them promise not to bring any. I have lived long among them and I know their strengths and weaknesses. I am no longer afraid of them, and I will not be on board when they leave our river." he assured them.

He moved away from his brothers toward the waiting Spanish priests. "Now, look hungry," he instructed them over his shoulder. "Remember, you have been living for many moons on roots and berries."

CHAPTER SEVEN

A Blow is Struck

When Opechancanough told this tale in the days of my childhood, he always shook his head ruefully when he got to that part, because his ruse did not work.

Lost Owl's eyes flash. "The Spanish didn't care." I nod. "The Jesuits were so convinced of the righteousness of their mission, and so sure that their god would look after them, that they sent their great canoe on its way back to Florida, and waited expectantly for Opechancanough to provide for them."

"The Spanish canoe just sailed away?" Savage Bear asks.

"Down the river and out the bay into the great ocean."

"Opechancanough must have been upset."

The youngsters are excited by the dilemma. "If their canoe had gone and there were only five priests," Savage Bear schemes, "Opechancanough could just get rid of them on the spot."

"Opechancanough's brothers suggested that he kill them, but he was grateful to the Jesuits for bringing him home. These were not the Spaniards who had kidnapped him, and they were sweet and gentle and kind to him. He had no quarrel with them and really didn't want to harm them."

45

Shad Running is eager to move the story along. "What did he do?"

Opechancanough was determined not to take the priests to his village or to any of the areas where the broad fields of dry cornstalks and bean plants and withered gourd vines surrounded the longhouses of his people. One of his brothers suggested that they take the Jesuits across the peninsula to a stretch of shore on the Pamunkey river where there were no villages. A small band of Chiskiak were camped there to harvest oysters; and Opechancanough's brothers thought they would welcome an offer of grain in exchange for letting the Spanish priests join their camp.

They rounded up canoes to make the transfer. The captain of the great Spanish canoe had left them a tub of tar to repair a crack in one of the canoes and a half barrel of flour that the priests would use to make bread.

Shad Running's face is skeptical. "They loaded the priests into canoes and paddled them down Powhatan's river and all the way back up the Pamunkey?"

"No, my son. You have never seen those broad rivers and that huge bay. The trip around the peninsula would have taken five days in deep water, so they went up the nearest creek to its source; then walked a short distance to the head of another creek, reloaded, and paddled down to our river. Then it was only a short distance along the shore to the cove where the Chiskiak had built their longhouses."

"They left them there?"

Opechancanough and his brothers built shelters for the Jesuits, using the axes, hammers, and nails that the priests had brought along. He had corn brought from afar for the priests and the Chiskiak to share. He left them and returned to his own village and a great celebration. He shed his Spanish clothes for the leather apron and necklaces of shell and animal teeth that all braves wore. The prettiest of the maidens vied for the privilege of shaping

his long hair into a forehead-to-neckline crest on top, with
one long hank over the left shoulder, and he immediately
chose a wife from among them.

The children stir and giggle at what seems like a happy
ending to the story—except they know that what must
have seemed to Opechancanough to be a perfect resolution
evolved eventually into tragedy. They press a little closer
to me on the mat, and their eager eyes urge me to go on.

The only thing that spoiled Opechancanough's happi-
ness at being back among his own people were the messages that kept coming up the trails from the Jesuit
priests. The Jesuits commanded him to return to them and
help them convert his people to the Spanish religion, as
they believed he'd promised to do. They sent word that
they were hungry, they were cold, they were wet, they
were ill, they needed him, they couldn't do their work
without him, they couldn't survive without him, and their
god was depending on him.

For the most part, he ignored them. It was not that he
didn't believe their complaints. It would soon be winter,
and he remembered the stands of palm trees and the azure
waters ringing their warm country, and knew that they
had no experience with snow or the sheet of ice that
stretched across the broad river until it crumpled in the
changing tide.

The nights were growing longer and crisper. As the
brilliant autumn leaves fell from the sour gums and sassa-
fras trees, gales blasted out of the northeast, whipping
over the river and into the clearings, whistling through
the chinks in the rough walls of their flimsy huts. The
Jesuits must have shivered in the cold dawns before the
sun burned off the mists and frost.

No grain was to be had then. Our people never tried to
keep corn from one season to the next, except for the seed
corn that hung in the arches over the fires. We knew how
fast the mold and insects would get it if we did not eat it.
When it was gone, we spread out into the forests and

hunted deer, rabbits, and wild turkey until spring came and we could plant again.

The priest in charge of the mission sent one brother after another on the long walk to Opechancanough's village to beg him to come to their rescue. Opechancanough's scouts kept track of their movements, and he always went out to meet the white men on the trail, before they reached his village.

They told him that they were praying every day that their god would again touch Opechancanough's heart and send him back to them. They must have prayed with gnawing bellies through the short, raw days when the trees were bare and the long nights when the winds howled. Opechancanough remembered that they celebrated the birthday of their god's son in this season. His people marveled at these strangers, stranded an ocean away from their homeland, surrounded by endless forest, but determined to bring to their god a tribe about whom they knew absolutely nothing. How could sheer faith sustain them against starvation and the biting winter cold?

As the weeks of the hunger moon dragged by, their food ran out completely. The priest in charge fell ill, and the others despaired. He felt that he had to make one more effort, and he sent three of the brothers to plead with Opechancanough to return and at least hunt for them so they would not starve.

The three spent the night in a Pasbehegh village, begging for corn. The next day, Opechancanough and some of his friends came to meet them on the trail.

Had they been wise—or even aware of the ways of our people—the Spaniards would not have said the things they did there in that leaf-strewn glade. Opechancanough admitted later that they spoke in desperation; but when it happened, he felt that they were shaming him before his companions and treating him like an ignorant child who should be at their beck and call. They scolded him for his ungrateful behavior and for falling from the grace he had been so privileged to receive from them.

Although the other braves could not understand the

Spanish words, the tone of the Jesuits' voices and their manner made it quite clear that they thought themselves his betters. Opechancanough stood on the forest path, on his own ground, a warrior born of a chief's family. Here, he wasn't a helpless captive to be ordered around at Spanish whim. Here, he was a prince in his own right, brave and respected, and a man to be reckoned with.

His control shattered when they told him that a great Spanish canoe would come any day, and it would be loaded with soldiers. If he didn't do as they told him, they would bring the soldiers to kill him and all of his tribe and burn their villages to the ground. He knew they didn't speak empty words, because he had seen this happen, again and again, in the southern islands where the Spanish had taken him in their great canoes.

The threats made that morning under bare oaks and sighing pines exploded Opechancanough's new sense of security and ended in disaster. To still their threats, he and his companions killed the three Jesuits on the spot. Before their rage had time to cool, they tramped on to the clearing where the others waited, and wiped out the Jesuit mission.

CHAPTER EIGHT

Revenge

"Except for the acolyte," Anne comments.

"Acolyte?" Lost Owl looks at her in puzzlement.

"The fifteen-year-old boy that they brought from Santa Elena.* He was born and grew up among our people far to the south, and he knew their language."

Lost Owl looks to me for confirmation.

"Anne remembers the story correctly. The Jesuits brought a youngster with them to help them with their religious ceremonies and in their dealings with our people. He learned our language much more quickly than the priests because he already knew that of the southland and was familiar with our ways. He was no longer with the Jesuits in their final moment of despair."

"What happened to him?"

"Once he had learned to talk with our people, he found out that the Kecoughtan band, living down at the very tip of the peninsula, had ample stores of food. He stole a hammer and some nails and knives from the Jesuit stores and sneaked off when they were not looking. He gave the tools to the Kecoughtan in exchange for permission to live with them and share their food."

---

*Now called Port Royal, South Carolina.

These boys, who are the same age as the Spanish boy we are discussing, look at each other and squirm on the mat as they debate in their own minds whether this action was cleverness or treachery.

Finally, one of them repeats, "What happened to him?"

The Kecoughtan had extended their hospitality to him, and he lived with them as their child through two more migrations of the geese. Then another great canoe pushed by the wind sailed between the capes, across the bay, and anchored at the mouth of Powhatan's river. The white men came ashore in their small boat with their thundersticks, and summoned our chiefs. When five of the chiefs came, they took them aboard the great canoe, demanding to know what had happened to the Spanish priests. Someone told them that the Spanish boy, Alonso, was living among the Kecoughtan. Word was imediately sent to our people that Alonso must be brought to the ship before our chiefs would be released.

Alonso was quickly produced, and the boy found himself face-to-face with the Spanish governor of Florida. The governor had stopped in our bay expressly to learn the fate of the Jesuits, because the Spanish supply ship that had come a *c'hunk* earlier had been greeted by a hail of arrows and departed without landing.

Alonso was afraid to admit that he had deserted the priests when the food ran out, so he lied and said that he had been with them all along. He claimed that Opechancanough had deserted them and given them no help whatsoever, and that he had come with his braves to the Jesuit settlement and slain them all—without any provocation—in cold blood.

Lost Owl is incensed at the falsehood. "How did Alonso explain the fact that he was still alive?"

Anne is engrossed in the contradiction and interrupts me. "He claimed that he begged the braves to kill him too, because he could not bear to live without the priests, but he was spared because the Kecoughtan chief loved him and rescued him."

The boys snort their disgust at the dissembling and slap their hands on the mat. Lost Owl urges me to go on.

The Spanish governor, after he had heard Alonso's story, sent word to our people that the chiefs would not be released until Opechancanough was brought to them to be punished for the killing of the Jesuit priests. Five days was the time allotted for him to appear.

"The Spanish actually thought that our people would surrender Opechancanough to them?" Savage Bear's fierce black eyes flash.

"They thought he would surrender himself," Anne explains, "to save the hostages. They didn't understand that that was not the way of our people. Our braves were not afraid to fight. If they died, they died without a whimper. In those days, we were strong and proud, and didn't surrender to an enemy. Not one of those captive chiefs would have expected Opechancanough to humiliate himself by placing himself again in Spanish captivity. After all, he had already been deprived of ten *c'hunks* of his young manhood."

"But the hostages were important chiefs," Shad Running argues.

"So was Opechancanough," Anne snaps. "Death in a fair fight to defend himself could have resolved it, but this sneaky Spanish trick to get their hands on Opechancanough— without giving him a chance to defend himself—deserved nothing but contempt. There was no way those chiefs would want their brother to give in to the Spanish, no matter how he agonized over the threat of their execution on the final day!"

I listen to the intensity in Anne's voice, and my heart is touched because she understands so well the code by which we lived. We have been driven and homeless for so long that now it is hard to remember how life could be shaped by honor among men and harmony with the spirits of Ahone who live in the forests and steams.

Anne turns to me, her forehead creased with concern that she has interrupted my story. I can only smile at her before I go on.

I try to imagine what those five days must have been like, with the whole landscape hushed in apprehension: no laughter, no singing, no sound of children's voices in any of the villages from the bay to the fall line. On the fifth day, the Spanish hanged the five chiefs from the yardarm of the governor's great ship, raised anchor, and sailed out of the bay.

We sit in silence for a long time, each of us measuring in our hearts the dimensions of this tragedy. This happened many *c'hunks* ago—long before I was born, and I am an old woman now. When I try to understand all that has happened to my people since then, it seems to me that those executions on the deck of the foreign ship were the beginning of all our troubles. Maybe the trouble began with Opechancanough's kidnapping twelve *c'hunks* earlier—even though his return from the dead was a cause for great rejoicing.

The Spanish governor destroyed the older, confident generation of leaders, forcing the younger braves to assume their mantles before they had been tested and gained wisdom. The painful knowledge of how fragile their power was haunted them ever after.

They were brave and strong and truly dedicated. Powhatan's son, Wahunsonacock, assumed his dead father's title as chief of the clan that lived at the fall line on Powhatan's river. Opechancanough had married a royal daughter of the Pamunkey line, making him eligible to succeed as chief of her people at Orapaks. Others stepped into the mocassins that the Spanish left empty, but they were all young men, with much still to learn. However, one grave lesson had already been learned: beware of the treachery of the white men who come from the rising sun out of the great ocean.

The chiefs posted sentinels on the capes and along the shores of the bay to watch for the great canoes pushed by the wind. Our priests tended the fires in Okee's temples at Orapaks and Uttamussak and made offerings imploring him to prevent further intrusions by the white foreigners.

Our people worried and waited.

CHAPTER NINE

A Frightening Prophecy

When Anne and the young people settle around me on the mat the next afternoon, there is a slip of a girl, Wind Sighing, among them. She is shy and quiet, just coming into her womanhood, and I am already aware that she is Lost Owl's favorite among the girl children his age. He guides her to a place beside him, where he can steal quick sideways glances at her as she sits demurely on her crossed legs, waiting for me to begin.

The other two boys are making jokes and showing off for her benefit, but she turns her almond-shaped eyes to the fire and pretends not to notice. As I study the firm skin so perfectly molded over the dainty cheekbones, the memory of myself and Totopotomoy at the same age flickers into my mind. A wave of nostalgia for that long ago time washes over me, and it requires a conscious effort to submerge it as I pick up the thread of my tale.

Okee listened to the prayers of our temple priests, and peace was on the land through twelve migrations of the geese. Our sentinels kept watch in their lonely stations on

the capes; but as moon followed moon, the memory of that day of Spanish retribution mellowed, and the young braves who had donned the chiefly mantles grew in experience and wisdom. They finally came to believe that the white men had gone back to wherever they had come from and would not trouble them again.

If not for Opechancanough, the vigil might have been abandoned; but his reminder was heard repeatedly around the council fires. He had lived among the Spanish and had traveled across the oceans with them to their own country. He knew how many great canoes pushed by the wind they sailed, and how great their lust was for the precious metals they had found in the lands to the south.

When word finally came of another arrival of the white men, it was not from our sentinels on the bay, but from a trader from the islands off the shores of our neighbors to the south. He came with a pack of seashells, which our women chipped into small discs for *peake.* He brought word that great canoes pushed by the wind had come to their coast, had gone ashore on the island they called Croatoa, and had departed after taking two Croatoan braves on board their ships.*

When he heard the news, Opechancanough nodded sagely and said to his companions, "You see? The threat is always there. It is only a matter of time before they will sail into our bay again." He asked the trader to tell his chief that we should be informed when the white men next appeared.

The leaves fell, the snows came, and the corn was standing tall in our gardens when a runner came with news from the south. The great canoes had returned with the two Croatoan braves, and a hundred white men had gone ashore to build shelters on the island they called Roanoke.**

---

*1583 in what is today called Cape Hatteras.
**1585.

Our braves listened with sinking hearts to tales of burned villages, robbed fish weirs, chiefs' sons held ransom for food, and whole villages threatened at gunpoint until they relinquished their grain stocks. The white men had searched up the rivers to the west and up the sound to the north for some passage through our country.

The visitor brought an invitation from his chief, Pemisapan, for our people to send someone to see with his own eyes what was happening. Pemisapan's father, who had welcomed the white men and planted corn for them, had just died. All of the neighboring chiefs were being summoned to his town on the mainland, across from Roanoke Island, for his funeral ceremonies. As they met to pay homage to the fallen *weroance,* they would have the opportunity to confer on their problems with the white men.

Lost Owl is excited and tries to hurry me. "Who went? Opechancanough?"

Opechancanough had already seen the white men in action. He wanted another of our chiefs to go and learn firsthand the threat they posed to our people. Powhatan's title was the most respected among our chiefs—five clans paid tribute to him even in those days. Opechancanough convinced the other chiefs that Powhatan should be the emissary to the conclave.

"He went?" The boys lean forward on their hands, mouths open in anticipation.

He went, and when he returned, he was sorely troubled and had a tragic tale to tell.

When the chiefs assembled in Pemisapan's village to sing the songs of death, the white men on Roanoke Island suspected that they were plotting treachery. As our men were meeting, the word came that two messengers who had been dispatched to the island near the chief's town had been tipped out of their canoe by English soldiers and murdered. Those on shore who saw the deed raised the alarm, and many braves rushed down to the water to shoot arrows at the white foreigners who were approaching in their barge. The foreigners immediately cocked their thundersticks, and three of our braves fell in pools of blood.

Chief Pemisapan quickly ordered all his guests to leave his village and hide in the forest, saying that he would negotiate with the white men. After he agreed that the English could come to his village, they cut him down where he stood, and carried his head away on a spike. Our people were horrified and stayed hidden in the sheltering forest.

Several days later, a great fleet of the canoes pushed by the wind arrived at the entrance to the sound. The foreigners who had been living on Roanoke Island hurried out in their small boats and went aboard the great vessels. For several days, there was much scurrying of white men between shore and ships.

Our people watched and waited.

Then a great storm roared in from the northeast, with forceful winds that bobbed the great canoes about like chips of bark in the water. The tides rose higher than the tallest man, and some of the small boats broke their moorings. The foreigners made haste to move away from the bars and shoals. The white men on shore struggled to free their own small boats, letting whatever burdened them plunge into the raging waves as they fought their way out to the great canoes. As soon as the gale caught the newly lofted sails, the great canoes scudded away with great speed and were lost from sight.

When the storm was over, the chiefs assembled to dance the litany of death around the sacred fire for both Pemisapan and his father. They hastily discussed the threat that had come out of the great ocean; then departed for their homelands to warn their own people.

The night of Powhatan's return, he and Opechancanough

conferred alone beside the fire, long after everyone else had gone to sleep.

They decided that the high priests should enlist the sanction of our guardian spirit Okee, who communicates with the Creator Ahone and all the spirits of nature. They would ask him for a prophecy that would strike fear into the hearts of all the chiefs up and down our rivers, so they would all take orders from the most able leader among them. That chief would take charge and combine the strength of all the bands, so they could stand up against any further invasion by the white men.

The next morning, runners were sent to all the villages along Powhatan's river and the Pamunkey river, instructing the chiefs to meet three days after the sighting of the next new moon in the temple at Orapaks where the most powerful of our ancestors were entombed.

The two schemers trekked overland to Orapaks ahead of the assembly date, while the nights were lighted only by the stars, to meet with the priests and to make plans for the ritual that was to produce the prophecy. There was some resistance to the ideas they outlined. The chief priest nodded sagely as they explained the danger; but when a federation of tribes was suggested, he protested. "Our people have never been commanded by one leader," he said.

"Have you forgotten what I learned in my travels?" Opechancanough argued. "The white men follow the commands of one king. We must take bold action if we are to be as strong as they. Our many small, divided bands cannot survive unless we work together."

There was much arguing back and forth, with Powhatan lending the weight of what he had seen at Roanoke. He was already an important chief, so the high priests listened politely to what he said. He and Opechancanough finally convinced them that this was no ordinary situation. Not only must the tribes cooperate, but the assistance of the supernatural was needed to convince the other leaders that this was the only way they could survive.

When the thin sliver of the crescent moon had slid three times across the evening sky, the chiefs from far and near were on the trails or pushing their canoes along the rivers with swift strokes in the direction of Orapaks. As they traveled toward the sacred meeting place, the priests prepared themselves and readied the temple for the day to come. The ritual attire that struck awe into the hearts of strong braves was brought out—the cloaks of many-colored bird feathers that would cover the revered shoulders, the collars of weasel skins that would encircle the priestly necks, the crowns of snakeskins stuffed with moss, tied by their tails into a peak that sat atop hair crests, encircled by a ruff of feathers. Hours were spent sitting patiently, while apprentices painted geometric designs with *puccoon juice* and walnut oil mixed with charcoal on dark cheeks, arms, and chests.

By this time, the other chiefs were reaching the temple and were receiving, as they stooped to push aside the mat that covered the door, the sacred drink that would make the statue of Okee move and speak during the ceremony. When all the braves were settled inside on woven mats arranged down the entire length of the longhouse, the fire on the hearth below the platform where the sacred statue sat was replenished, and the priests began their chants at the doorway.

One by one, they came prancing in weaving a procession down the center aisle, shaking their gourd rattles and rotating their heads to make the snakeskins whirl. They were accompanied by conjurers waving tall fronds of feathery marsh grass. Each wore a small, stuffed blackbird perched on one ear as a symbol of his office. Jugglers moved on the edge of the procession, clicking wooden snappers, tossing balls, and swinging knotted cords in tight patterns. All of them were chanting and singing, and by the time they reached the mats around the fire, the chorus had reached a crescendo.

The invocations were lengthy so Okee could speak to the Creator Ahone, who made the earth and the sky and taught our people how to plant the many kinds of corn that give us nourishment. The longhouse grew close and hot from the press of the many bodies and the exertions of the conjurers and jugglers circling the fire. Smoking pipes were passed from mouth to mouth, drinking bowls from hand to hand, and brands were tossed on the fire whenever it dwindled. The air grew heavy with smoke, and sweat poured off the swaying bodies. When it seemed as if they would all faint from the heat, or that the din would split open the throbbing heads of the spectators, the chief priest gave a sudden signal. The leaping clergy turned in sharp unison to face the platform, and the chants and songs ceased so abruptly that the interior of the steamy, smokey hall seemed to quiver in the unexpected silence.

The chief priest moved in tense, crouching steps to the platform and spoke in a sacred tongue to the sitting god. As the braves hung breathlessly on the mysterious syllables, the statue flexed its muscles and rose from the platform to hang suspended in the air. It spoke to the assembly in slow, measured, incomprehensible sounds whispered out of the shadows overhead. The priests listened intently, while the braves trembled and some hid their faces in awe. When the chief priest turned and raised his arms toward the ceiling, Okee sank slowly back to his place on the platform.

The chief priest translated the god's message in a powerful voice that seemed to shake the very mats that walled the longhouse. "Okee has spoken a warning—a prediction that invaders will come out of the east, intent on destroying the people of our rivers. Three times, they will come. Twice our people will repel the strangers; but on the third time, the invaders will plant their roots in our soil and they will drive our braves, our women, and our children forever from our ancestral homes."

CHAPTER TEN

Building Strength

Lost Owl is so dismayed by the prophecy that he springs to his feet and paces around the perimeter of the longhouse. He is tall for his age, with long agile legs, steady hands, and a marksman's eye. I have great hopes that he will stand by his mother's side when I am gone and she succeeds me.

"Did the chiefs believe the prophecy?" he demands.

Opechancanough, who had planned the ceremony, was furious. All he had wanted was something to unite the bands under one leader. Instead, he got a forecast of doom, witnessed by all the chiefs from far and near. There was no way to keep the prediction from spreading among all the people along the rivers. Even if the chiefs worked together to repel the first and second invasions, how could they muster opposition to the third invasion when Okee had already predicted that they would be vanquished?

"If they thought about it," Anne comments, "the Spanish Jesuits who brought Opechancanough home were the first, and the English at Roanoke Island were the second invasion."

"Exactly. The next appearance of the great canoes pushed by the wind would be the third invasion." Lost Owl turns back to me, his unanswered query etched in the scowl between his brows.

I smile inwardly at his intensity and assure him that Opechancanough berated the chief priest for making such a negative prophecy. When he demanded to know what they were to do, however, the priest shrugged his shoulders and said that it wasn't his responsibility. He made the charms, cast the spells, and conjured up the prophecies, and the chiefs would have to live with what they had gotten.

"What did they do?" Shad Running asks anxiously, chewing at a hangnail on his forefinger.

Opechancanough and Powhatan agonized over the question of what to do for many weeks. They finally decided to follow two courses of action. The first was that Powhatan should marry a princess from each of the bands up and down our two rivers. Each princess would stay with him until she produced a son; then she would return to her band. Because the royal line passes through the women of our tribes, her son would become the next chief of the band. Every clan would then be allied with Powhatan by his own royal blood.

Opechancanough then convinced Powhatan that his village at the fall line on his river was too far inland and not central enough for him to command the obedience of all the chiefs. Powhatan eventually put a son in charge of that village, and he established a new headquarters in a more central location, halfway down the main course of the Pamunkey river.

"Werowocomoco—residence of the high chief," Anne murmurs. She remembers that famous name, even though the village was abandoned about the time that I was born.

Shad Running, who is a worrier by nature, is not satisfied with the decisions I have described. "Why didn't Opechancanough marry the princesses and become the supreme chief? He's the one who knew the most about the white men. If he had been chief when the English came to Jamestown, he would never have let them land their canoes, and we would have been spared all our troubles."

I myself have often wondered if the outcome might have been different if Opechancanough had been in charge when those three English ships sailed up Powhatan's river. The traditional arrangements for tribal leadership ordained otherwise.

Opechancanough was of the Chickahamen tribe, who lived in the central interior of the peninsula. Unlike all the other bands that lived on the river's edge, the Chickahamen were ruled by a council of chiefs, with no single brave in a superior position. Powhatan, in contrast, not only controlled his own clan, but five other clans had pledged their allegiance to his father before his death. Thus, the ground was fertile for expansion of his tributaries into an alliance. Opechancanough believed that the alliance had to be forged before the white men appeared again, and he realized that the essential unity could be accomplished more speedily under Powhatan's leadership than under his own.

"And that's what happened," Anne comments. "Powhatan built a new town called Werowocomoco and married his princesses. Within twenty migrations of the geese, every band from the capes to the fall line on his river and on the Pamunkey river had sworn allegiance to his authority and sent tribute for his storehouses."

"So then they called him Great Powhatan." Lost Owl sinks back onto the mat. His eyes are dreamy as he unconsciously lifts the end of a thick braid from Wind Sighing's arm and wraps the black hair around his finger. "He was the greatest chief our people have ever known."

"Except for Opechancanough," his mother reminds him.

"But Opechancanough brought us nothing but trouble," the boy protests. "You all speak of Powhatan's rule as one that we can be proud of—one of greatness and peace."

"Greatness, yes. But peace? Not completely. We remember Powhatan's rule as peaceful because he refused to be drawn into open warfare with the white men. But there were troubles and danger, and Powhatan was sorely tried by the decisions he was forced to make. That is, however, getting ahead of the story."

The geese flew south and returned twice after Powhatan's return from Roanoke Island; then word came that a hundred white men—including a few women and children this time—had been put ashore on Roanoke Island by great canoes pushed by the wind.* The vessels then weighed anchor, sailed back into the sunrise, and disappeared. The newcomers built shelters, surrounded by a strong palisade, but that protection was not sufficient. All of the tribes in the area were hostile after what had happened to Pemisapan. The white men had to have food, and they had to leave the safety of their palisade to secure it. They had arrived too late to plant crops themselves, and our people refused to supply them—except under duress. To fish and hunt, they had to move far from the security of their fort, and the new chief, Wingina, harassed them at every opportunity.

Before very long, the newcomers abandoned their new settlement—loading up their small boats and heading north up the sound—leaving behind a handful of soldiers to guard their heavy stores. English explorers made that same trip north two *c'hunks* earlier, and encountered the southernmost village of the Chesapeac tribe, where they had been welcomed. Some of the explorers had remained throughout a summer and fall among the Chesapeac, and trusted their friendship.

---

*1587.

It appeared that the new group of white men were
headed for Chesapeac country. After some moons, one of
our braves visited the Chesapeac, and reported that the
English settlers had indeed moved north and were living
peacefully in the Chesapeac village called Skicoak.

Lost Owl interrupts, "Where is Skicoak?"

I assure him that it is a good day's journey by foot from
the south shore of the bay up a tributary river that flows
out of the south. The Chesapeac preferred to remain in
the interior, rather than occupying the shore of the bay.
Their other principle village, Chesapeac, was also a day's
journey inland, located on another inlet that flows out of
the south.

He is puzzled. "Were the Chesapeac included in Powhatan's
federation?"

"Not by royal marriage."

Because they chose to live deep in the forests rather
than on our shores, and were a peaceful people, Powhatan
did not consider them to be a threat. Even when he
learned that the white men were living with them, he did
not think of them as invaders. He and his council decided
that we were in no danger from the Roanoke settlers
unless and until more English canoes came from the ocean
and discovered them among the Chesapeac. Instead,
Powhatan went about consolidating his authority over as
many of the nearer villages as possible.

The first alarm, however, was not long delayed. Word
came that very winter from Powhatan's sentinels on both
capes that a great canoe pushed by the wind had sailed
into the bay. Men went ashore on the south bank to take
on fresh water, but they made no contact with the
Chesapeac; then they sailed away again. Because Powhatan had not yet welded his forces strongly enough
to counter any threat from the great ocean, everyone in
Werowocomoco was very nervous following the report of
this visit.

The following summer, a new alarm sounded. Another great canoe appeared, and its actions puzzled Powhatan's council. It made a speedy reconnaissance north up the entire length of the bay, sailed back down the eastern shore, and then departed without making any contact with the Chesapeac.

Powhatan's lookouts watched and wondered and were again left to themselves. The days lengthened into moons. Twelve more migrations of the geese passed before another great canoe appeared, and this one sailed north up the bay to the country of the Rappahannoc tribe.*

In Werowocomoco, Powhatan knew of its arrival as it passed between the capes, and scouts watched as a strong southwest wind billowed the great sails steadily upstream. When it moved, at last, out of the wide bay and into the quieter waters of the Rappahannoc river, Opechancanough moved swiftly.

"This great canoe has not arrived here by accident," he announced to Powhatan's council. "Its movements are very purposeful. We must destroy the English settlers who live among the Chesapeac before it returns down the bay and makes contact with them."

"How can we destroy the English without making war on the Chesapeac, who are their hosts?" Powhatan argued.

"If the Chesapeac choose to fight in defense of the white men, then we must make war on the Chesapeac as well."

Runners went out to all the villages up and down both rivers, and the chiefs were commanded to stand immediately to support Powhatan. They streamed with their braves out of their clearings, shoved their canoes into the stream toward the sun (as the spirits demand), and paddled swiftly to the south shore of the bay.

Powhatan mustered them into a fighting company, gave them instructions, and sent them on the trail. The attack was swift and bloody, particularly effective because neither the Chesapeac nor the English had any inkling of

---

*1598.

the sudden menace that shot out of the west. Two set-
tings of the sun, and it was over. The English were wiped
out, and a large share of the Chesapeac braves fell with
them. Those who survived were warned to never again
give shelter to any white men and were bound into
tribute to Great Powhatan. A company of Powhatan's
braves was appointed to remain and rule Chesapeac
country.

As the others rested on the southern shore after their
mission was completed, the foreign canoe came sailing back down the bay and moved out into the vast
eastern ocean. Our people watched and pondered its
purpose. When they arrived back in Werowocomoco,
the chief of the Rappahannoc tribe was there awaiting
them.

"We received these strangers politely, and gave them
food," he told Powhatan, "and they repaid our kindness by
kidnapping two of my braves whom they caught out in a
canoe. They have taken them and sailed away. I know not
where."

Opechancanough was jubilant. "You see? That is exactly what happened to me. The white men are taking
your braves back to their own country, where they will
be taken from place to place and exhibited like ani-
mals."

"Are we forced to submit meekly to the whim of these
white invaders?" the Rappahannoc chief demanded.

Powhatan told him then how he and his allies had just
destroyed a whole group of white men who had been living
among the Chesapeac, how he intended to do everything
in his power to protect his people, and how he was
building alliances with all the chiefs in tidewater, so
they could act in concert against this menace from beyond
the seas.

"Then we will join you," the Rappahannoc chief announced without hesitation. "My braves will stand ready

to do your bidding whenever new danger arises. We will send deer skins and *peake* and copper to signify our allegiance to your cause."

CHAPTER ELEVEN

Preparing for Manhood

A spattering of rain blows across the clearing, rattling the mats over our heads. Old Woman has drifted off to sleep. "Why don't we wait until another day," Anne whispers, "to continue our recitation?"

The faces of the young people are washed with expressions of surprise at the quick passage of time. They stand and stretch and leave the circle with some reluctance. "We want to be here when you continue the story," Lost Owl admonishes me. I promise to wait for them.

With an unexpected sense of elation over their interest in what I have to tell them, I watch them wander toward the door. Perhaps I have been wrong in thinking that my people are too weary and defeated to care about the days when this whole land was ours. Perhaps these tales should have been told many times since Opechancanough's death.

In the old days, a chosen few among the priests were trained during their *huskenaw* to recount our history when we were all gathered on a festive occasion around the evening fires. I heard them many times in my youth, and I am amazed at how much of it came back to me as I sat tonight with Old Woman, Anne, and the youngsters.

Those orators of my childhood are all dead now. Times

have been too troubled, and our priesthood too decimated, to carry on the initiation ceremonies that would have prepared orators—even in Anne's generation. It was hard enough for the braves to teach their sons to hunt and fight.

The rapt attention of these boys and lovely little Wind Sighing reminds me of how much we have lost by abandoning the old traditions. The first uprising interrupted our lives before I reached initiation age, and we have been refugees ever after. The older women taught us the household arts—how to weave mats and baskets, to shape pots from clay so they sit erect in the fire, to tan rawhide with hot animal brains, to beat tendons and sinew into fine twine, to cut gourds into water containers, to grow corn, and to bear our children with quiet fortitude. But my generation never had its testing time together, alone, out in the forest.

My older brother, Anne's father, was one of the fortunate ones whose *huskenaw* was completed while we still lived at Orapaks. He was of the right age just a few seasons before the uprising, and I remember how awed I was when he left our family in the long ceremony of mourning that symbolized spiritual death. He and the boys in his age group were given a drink made from the fresh roots of the spreading dogbane. It made them delerious, so they would entirely forget the years they had been children. They built a sapling lodge in the forest, and lived there with the priests who were trained to initiate them into manhood through the season when the earth sleeps.

When Anne and the youngsters gather again, I ask them if they would like me to tell them what my brother told me about his *huskenaw*—how they fasted to humble and weaken themselves, how they swam in the icy streams, how they underwent every kind of ordeal to test their courage and endurance, and how they learned to bear extreme discomfort and pain without whimpering. The priests taught them the tribal lore and history and saw to it that they learned it all by heart.

Anne's voice softens with longing. "Oh yes, please."

When my brother, Anne's father, came back home after his *huskenaw,* the season of rebirth was truly appreciated after the misery and testing the boys had endured. They came naked from their hidden place in the forest in the dawn of the morning following the first sighting of the new moon. Each one proudly carried a fine bow of ash wood, carefully crafted and balanced during the long weeks of seclusion. Each had hung over his shoulder a new leather quiver of perfect arrows—their flint points as sharp as the edge of a marsh frond and their shafts absolutely straight and perfectly balanced by tiny feathers tied tightly with mulberry bark strips. That took hours of patient work.

Savage Bear snorts and moves restlessly on the mat. He is a heavy, stocky boy, who bullies his playmates and reacts sullenly to discipline. He is proud of the jagged scar that seams his shoulder.

I remind him that every brave—even the mightiest chief—took pride in his own hand-crafted arrows.

"Who wants to hunt with arrows?" he protests. "The English guns are the way to bring down a deer." He rises to his knees and goes through the motions of loading and firing a blunderbuss. Shad Running crouches beside him, rapt with the toughness of his companion.

"I agree that English guns are quick and efficient and give the hunter an enormous sense of power. But what about the deer?" I ask.

Savage Bear peers around at me, his small eyes squinting.

"We don't kill the deer because we are angry with him," I remind him. "We kill him because we need food to eat and skins for clothing and blankets. We tell Ahone we are sorry to have to destroy one of his creatures. The deer runs as a free spirit in the forest too, and his death should

not be so easy that it is done for the excitement of killing. The gun robs the deer of his dignity. If it makes his killing a casual thing, requiring little skill or effort or planning on the hunter's part; then how can the deer be brave and confident?"

"The English use their guns against us," Savage Bear snaps. "Are the deer any better than we are?"

In the tense silence that hangs on his question, we hear the rattle of an acorn as it drops from limb to limb in a tree outside. I shake my head, because there is no answer to the boy's challenge.

"Tell us what happened when my father came home from his *huskenaw*." Anne senses my dilemma and draws me back to my tale.

All of the families in the village stayed hidden in our longhouses as the boys, led by their priests, filed down to the river's edge. They looked like strange spirits from another world, for each one had blackened his head and chest with charcoal and oil in the image of death.

The boys laid their bows and quivers in a circle around the fire burning in front of the sacred longhouse. The priests took their places around the fire as their leader began a slow, mournful chant. The boys moved down into the water, scooping up handfuls of sand. As the head priest recited the story of creation, death, and immortality, the boys scrubbed away their black masks in the icy water. It required vigorous rubbing with the sand to get rid of the oily covering, causing their skin to glow hot and red like babies when they were finally clean.

The sun had topped the trees when the last boy left the river, reclaimed his bow and quiver, and took his place in the larger circle around the priests. The chant ended, and the silence that fell on the village was so intense that the chirping of awakening birds vibrated in the trees.

Then, on a signal from the head priest, all the boys lifted their heads and gave the two great shouts of greeting that we use for any meeting of friends. As the echoes rippled

through the forest, the boys' fathers pushed aside the
entrance mats of their longhouses, each carrying a leather
apron and strings of beads and shells. They filed into a
third circle and presented them to the boy behind whom
they stopped. When the apron was fastened at the youth's
waist, the necklaces were draped around his neck. The
father didn't try to identify his own son, because the boys
were no longer the children who had gone into the forest
the previous fall. They came back as adults with new
names and identities, and our families had to pretend not
to know them.

Another signal from the priest evoked the double shout
from all three circles of men; then all the women and girls
and small boys came tumbling out of the longhouses,
shouting joyous greetings of welcome and celebration.

We formed a fourth circle around the fire, and the
hubbub gradually died down. The mothers, who had more
difficulty pretending not to know their children than the
fathers, were devouring their sons with their eyes. The
young men looked so different with the loose hair of
boyhood clipped into the forehead-to-neckline crest, and a
forelock tied on the left side. My brother had grown at
least half a hand during his time in the forest, and his
crest made him appear even taller. I was bursting with
pride because he stood among the tallest of them.

When it was quiet again, our chief Opechancanough
joined the head priest in the center of the circles beside the
fire, and the naming ritual began. Each youth had a
sponsor among the priests who brought him to the center
of the ring and told how he had responded to his testing
and the name that had been selected as right for him to
carry throughout his manhood.

After each had been named, he lifted his bow, nocked
one of his arrows against the string, and shot it with all of
his strength into the glow of the rising sun. After the
ceremonies ended, any uninitiated girl who found an ar-
row in the forest could claim its maker as her protector
until she married.

Wind Sighing ducks her head and smiles up sideways at Lost Owl. The muscles tighten around his mouth.

When the sun was overhead, the braves led us to the dance circle, where the priests began the drum beat and the young men who had just returned from their *huskenaw* paced out the powerful circles of the creation dance. When the echoes finally died away in the forest, everyone was hungry because the lean months of winter were just behind us and the gardens were not yet planted. On a hearth at the other end of the village, a row of dressed geese were roasting on spits. This feast was the first of the springtime and was provided by a hunting excursion into the marshes the previous day. It touched all of us with joy because the season of rebirth was upon us and our sons and brothers were in our midst again.

Anne's father grew into a powerfully built and handsome man, and he became an expert tracker. I am sad that she never knew him. She was a child of his middle age, and he died with Opechancanough in the second uprising—just before she was born.

Then there is a lump in my throat that stops my speaking. My memories are so thickly populated with the ranks of my people—the Pamunkey were once as numerous as the Chickahamen. I have accepted the disappearance of my mothers, fathers, brothers, and sisters by hiding them far away in the corners of my mind where the measure of their loss can be kept separate from the aches and frustrations of each passing day.

Have I been wrong in carrying the burden of all this tragedy hidden in my heart?

It seems to me that the handful of my people who have survived might be crushed by any honest calculation of how far we have strayed from our heritage and how much we have lost. The temples of our most powerful spirit have been destroyed, and we have no substitute in their place.

If we cannot even provide Lost Owl and his companions with the teachers to lead them through their *huskenaw,* how can we expect them to translate pride in their past into a sense of purpose for the future? Yet this afternoon, as they surround me on the mat, their faces are eager and their eyes are demanding as they hear what I have to say.

I was born just before the Peace of Pocahontas began, and Old Woman and I are the only ones left now who remember that long-ago time. I must plan carefully what more I shall tell these youngsters, because I am the only thread that links them to the chiefs of those bygone days. When they have heard my tale, they will decide whether any of our experience can mark the trails through the troubled times ahead.

CHAPTER TWELVE

Lost Owl's Fury

Before we meet again to share the lore of our tribe, my son John West rides into our village.

Since he has grown to manhood, he has spent more and more of his time in the settlements of the English colony— especially since the ceremony five *c'hunks* ago, when the governor gave him the beautiful English clothes and weapons sent by King Charles. Our longhouses and cooking fires seem primitive to him when compared to the sturdy English houses of wattle and brick. Our leather skirts and rabbit skin capes embarrass him, and he thinks we are silly to hunt with bows and arrows, to hone shell scrapers, and to throw clay pots, when we know the power of the English guns and knives.

He is right about the English tools, of course, and we would all love to have them. But there is a high price in service to the white men that must be paid before they dole out any of their guns and metal knives to us. Even when the price is fully paid, they are not generous. My braves who served as guides and warriors for the white men have English weapons, but not enough ammunition to hunt with them. The powder horns were doled out piecemeal as they trekked through the forests with the

81

militia. Bacon and his men stole everything else of value that we had accumulated over the years. If there are skins to be cured, and no English knives to scrape them, then we must use the flint and shell that our people have always used.

John West is wearing an English shirt and breeches when he comes, and he has let his hair grow long in the foreign style. With his pale skin and strangely luminous eyes that are the color of hickory nuts, he resembles his English father far more than he resembles me.

It is hard to talk with him because he is so quick to find fault with everything we do and say; and when I look at him, he seems more like a stranger than a child of mine. Oddly enough, his presence keeps me harking back to memories of the two boys I bore to Totopotomoy so many years ago. They died so very young of the disease the English call smallpox. Their tiny forms are almost dreamlike to me now, yet the haughty bearing of my only living child suddenly evokes images of the braves they might have become had they grown to manhood.

Lost Owl and Wind Sighing find me sitting in the warm afternoon sunlight with John West and Anne, who is weaving a basket. "When will you talk again to us of Great Powhatan and Opechancanough?" the boy asks innocently.

John West snorts. "What are you telling them? How our great chiefs bungled all their relations with the English and then tried to wipe them out?"

Lost Owl is startled by the mocking tone in John West's voice, and his mother answers, "Cockacoeske is telling the boys our tribal history, so it will not be forgotten."

Wind Sighing begins to move away, but Lost Owl catches her wrist, almost unconsciously, and holds it easily as he faces John West.

"Better to forget it—it's a sorry story." My son speaks to Anne, but I can see those cynical pale eyes registering the obvious affection Lost Owl feels for the slender girl beside him.

"There are those of us who prefer to remember," Anne answers crisply and turns her attention back to the half-woven basket. It hangs suspended, bottom up, from a tree limb, and the strips of mulberry bark that she is weaving into it lie in a pile by her side.

"What is the point in remembering?" John West argues, picking his nose with a dirty fingernail. "Everything that the English have—their weapons, their tools, their clothes, their way of building houses—is better than yours. They know how to forge metal and make glass from sand and slice trees into boards. They build great ships that cross the ocean and construct brick buildings that withstand the storms. They have books in which they write the instructions for all the marvelous things they can do. Their god is omnipotent, while Okee and his silly spirits are helpless idols. You would be better off forgetting the past and learning the English ways as quickly as possible so you can live as they do."

"You think we should go live with the English?"

"I find staying at Middle Plantation very pleasant."

"Ah, but you are the Queen of Pamunkey's son and are given special privileges. If the rest of us wanted to live with the English, they would put us to work in their tobacco fields beside their black slaves."

John West merely grunts.

John West's arrogance annoys Anne. "If we go to live in the English villages," she snaps, "they would want us to sit all day sewing inside a stuffy house, or hoe all day in the rows of a garden. They disapprove of our going off to hunt or fish—and even of our children running free through the forest. They disapprove of everything we do. We mustn't let our hair grow long as they do because they want to be able to identify us immediately. They are disgusted when we grease our skin to ward off mosquitos, or bare our bodies in the summer heat. They fine us for resting in the shade and beat us for lying down together. How can we live like that?"

Lost Owl listens to this exchange with serious dark eyes.

Because John West is my son and Anne is my brother's daughter, they call each other brother and sister. Lost Owl should call John West his father, but he never does. He knows, just as I do, that Anne neither likes nor trusts John West. As I study the slightly condescending sneer on my son's face, I realize that I don't like or trust him either. I love him because he is my own flesh and blood, but I would know a greater serenity today had I never met his English father.

John West has no answer to Anne's challenge. He pushes himself brusquely off the mat and snaps, "You are all such simpletons!" as he strides away.

Lost Owl leans over and gently rubs his mother's shoulder as he watches John West's departure. The gesture is completely unconscious, but it must be comforting to Anne. It occurs to me that it is time that we gave Lost Owl a man's title and stopped calling him by the child's name he was given when a small barred owl perched on the arch of Anne's longhouse the night he was born.

"John West will not stay with us long," Anne tells her son and the dainty girl beside him as she slides another strip of bark into her basket frame. "When he leaves us again, Cockacoeske will go on with her story."

The next morning, I discover that he has left during the night, and only then does it become clear why he paid us this brief visit. Savage Bear and Shad Running have slipped away with him in the darkness, leaving Lost Owl to inform their parents the next day.

It seems that another clergyman has been sent from London with instructions to start a school to educate our people in the English ways. This has been going on ever

since I was born, but as far as I know, Chanco, Pocahontas,
and one or two others were the only ones able to accept
the English teachings completely enough to become one of
them. Others of our people have tried briefly, but the focus
of the teachings is always on the English god and the son
they call Jesus; and learning to read and write requires
an unquestioning acceptance of those gods.

Some of our young people have tried to take that enormous leap, but the reading and writing require sitting for
many hours in closed rooms, copying strange marks on slate,
then recognizing them when they appear in the English
books. It is a tedious discipline for children who have
spent their entire lives roaming over meadows and forests
and streams. They soon become impatient with the cramped
precision of these lessons and abandon them when the
gull's call or the wind in the treetops beckons them.

John West has come with promises of fine clothes and a
sharp hunting knife to entice our boys to go with him to
Middle Plantation and start their lessons. Why it had to
be done in secret—without even my knowledge—I cannot
understand. I am annoyed with him for going around my
authority. I suppose he knew that the youngsters' parents
would have strong objections; but I would have insisted
that the matter be fairly discussed with the boys if he had
approached me openly about his mission.

It is done now, but Lost Owl is downcast by the disappearance of his friends. His mother shakes her head in
annoyance and tells him not to grieve. They will soon
tire of the tasks the English priest sets them to do, and
they will slip away to return to us as quietly as they
departed.

Then we discover that an even heavier blow has fallen—
one that turns Lost Owl's sorrow to fury. John West has
taken not only the two boys with him, but Wind Sighing
has also slipped away—at his urging—to live with an
English tobacco planter, who promised a cloth blouse,

skirt, and a silver bracelet to a maiden willing to brighten his forest clearing.

Lost Owl's first impulse is to go after her, but Anne restrains him. "You'll get shot if the Englishman finds you on his property!"

"Are we to let him have Wind Sighing?" he rages.

"She went of her own accord. You have no assurance that she would return, even if you did track her down." Anne is certain that Wind Sighing will soon tire of cooking and hoeing and will return on her own.

"She will lie with the white man!" He spits out the words.

"It's too late to prevent that," Anne points out.

The boy paces angrily up and down the length of the longhouse as they argue, his anguished eyes focused anywhere but on his mother or me. I watch the rippling muscles in his legs and broad shoulders, his whole body tightened with the tension of his anger; and I can almost see in that taut figure the powerful man that he will soon become.

When Anne coaxes him to come to the mat and let my story-telling take his mind off his troubles, Lost Owl clamps his lips together in an angry scowl and kneads his fists.

"I will wait a day or two," he announces finally, "but if she doesn't return by then, I will go after her and bring her back by force."

CHAPTER THIRTEEN

When the Great Canoes Came

Powhatan had sired a hundred sons. Some of them had grown to manhood before the great canoes came again to his river. There were three of them this time, and they landed first on the south shore in Chesapeac country.*

After two days, they crossed the mouth of the river and disembarked among the Kecoughtan, who received them politely. Powhatan's son Pochins was chief, and although he offered his visitors trenchers of venison, smoked oysters, and succotash as our rules of hospitality require, he followed the feast with a dance to assure the spirits that his people would defend their village.

For several days, English exploring parties scoured the shores upriver. They called at the mouth of the Chickahamen tributary, where the Pasbehegh chief Wowinchopunk entertained them, but then asked them to go away. They crossed the river and visited a *weroance* on the southern shore. Their small exploring boat went farther upstream, where the Appamattucs permitted them to land, but did not conceal their hostility.

Finally, the three ships returned downstream and moored

*1607.

87

beside an island in the river where cypress trees grew beside deep water along the shore. This was Pasbehegh country. When word went up the forest paths to Wowinchopunk, he was not the least bit happy to hear about this invasion of his ancestral hunting grounds.

A few days later, he sent a party of a hundred Pasbehegh braves, bearing a deer as a gift, to find out what the white men were doing on his island.* While there, one of the braves picked up a hatchet that was lying on a tree stump—the first he had ever seen—to examine it, and an Englishman snatched it back. A scuffle ensued, the English grabbed their muskets in a threatening manner, and the Pasbehegh retreated in angry confusion.

They reported to Wowinchopunk that the white men had erected shelters out of a material that looked like deerskin, but wasn't, and were offering beads, metal tools, and copper trinkets in exchange for corn and wild game. Soon, Pasbehegh from all over the area were paddling their canoes, laden with the yields of their gardens and hunting expeditions, to the island to exchange them for the fascinating foreign glitter.

Before many days had passed, another exploring party led by two of the white chiefs, Captain Christopher Newport and Captain John Smith, sailed up the river as far as the rapids. Reports were that Captain Newport was a *weroance* of mature years, who had earned his status and lost an arm in mighty battles; but Captain Smith was a young man, at the peak of his fighting prowess. They were kindly received by the chiefs of the Arrahattucs, the Appomattucs, and by Powhatan's son Parahunt near the rapids at his town called Powhatan. Powhatan no longer lived there, having moved his headquarters to a more central location on the Pamunkey river. The English were confused by the fact that Parahunt was called

---

*Now Jamestown Island.

Tanx Powhatan, "Little Powhatan," and they treated him
with great honor.

While the white men were exploring, Chief Wowinchopunk
gathered, from among his own Pasbeheghs his friends the
Quioughcohannoc, the Weyanoc, the Appamattucs, and the
Chiskiak, a war party of several hundred braves to make a
show of force that would convince the newcomers that they
were not welcome on his island. The Englishmen rallied
behind the crude defensive palisade that they had erected
around their tiny tent village, and finally drove the
Pasbehegh off by firing the big guns on their ships—but
not before two of the white men had been killed and
several others injured.

Other attacks followed, but the English hastily constructed
a stout fortification of logs around their settlement. Captain John Smith supervised the building of a palisade
stronger than any other our people had seen, and the
Pasbeheghs soon realized that Smith was the English war
chief.

In the middle of the hottest season—to the great surprise of the sentinels posted to watch the settlement—
the two larger vessels were loaded up and sailed down
the river out into the ocean. The smallest of the canoes
pushed by the wind and over a hundred of the white men
remained.

As the growing season wore on, the Pasbehegh sentinels
saw fewer and fewer of the Englishmen. They wondered
how they were surviving when there was no good drinking
water on the island. When the time for the harvest of the
second corn crop came, our people realized that the foreigners were hungry. Captain John Smith sailed his barge
down to the Kecoughtan village at the end of the peninsula, ran it ashore, and chased the Kecoughtan braves into
the woods with muskets. He stole their statue of Okee
from the temple. To get it back, they had to fill his boat
with corn, venison, and turkey.

Twice, John Smith sailed up to Chickahamen country

and bargained there for food. The days were shortening and the nights were growing cool. The dogwoods and sour gum trees blazed crimson against the green hollies and pines. Acorns were dropping noisily from tall tree crowns, and squirrels ran industriously to and fro, collecting their winter hoard. It was the time of the final harvest, but the Englishmen had planted no gardens—not that anything would have grown in the slimy clay soil of the island where they were camped.

The harvest was over and most of the Chickahamen were out on deer sweeps when Captain John Smith sailed again up their river. The old people left in the villages watched as his barge shoved past them, up the steadily narrowing channel, between the broad marshes and the low, flat thickets of scrub. Finally, he went so far upstream that he left Chickahamen country and moved into Pamunkey hunting territory.

When his barge could go no farther, he tied it up and left some of his men there with it. He and two of his companions hired two Chickahamen braves as guides and transferred into their canoe. They paddled upstream as far as the canoe would go, poling against the gentle current through the shallows, fallen logs, and marshy bogs, and pushing aside the grass and debris that impeded their passage. Finally, they beached the canoe. Leaving the two Englishmen and one of the guides to prepare food, Smith and the other guide started to follow the narrow stream on foot.

They had not gone far when they encountered a Pamunkey hunting party. John Smith tied his wrist to the guide's and started to retreat, but our people were all around him by that time. He loaded and fired his pistol as fast as he could while backing up with his guide held in front of him. The guide was talking with the attackers, who insisted that all of Smith's men left with the barge had been killed, and that he must lay down his arms if he wished to live.

In the midst of the confusion, Captain Smith continued

to edge back toward the canoe with his eyes glued on his attackers, until he stepped unwittingly off solid ground into the slippery mud of the swamp. Losing his balance, he fell flat on his back, dragging his guide down on top of him. There they lay, mired and unable to rise without risking a hail of probably fatal arrows from the circle facing them as they struggled to regain their footing.

The Englishman finally accepted the hopelessness of his situation, and tossed his gun onto the dry ground.

I glance at Lost Owl and find his eyes are still fierce and brooding. Nothing I could say would console him, so I go on.

That was how the English war chief came to be the prisoner of Opechancanough, who was by then chief of the Pamunkey. John Smith was the only one of the white men who seemed to have any idea of how to survive in our forests and the only really brave man among them. Opechancanough always said that if he had only killed him then—even without Powhatan's approval—everything might have been different.

Lost Owl growls, "Why didn't he?"

"Opechancanough said that because John Smith was a *weroance,* the law of the tribe forbade disposing of him without consulting Great Powhatan; so he sent a messenger to Werowocomoco, asking permission to kill the English chief."

"Powhatan should have agreed."

Powhatan sent word that if Captain Newport returned with the other great canoes and found his war chief dead, he might be very angry and turn his big guns on our villages. His instructions were to hold John Smith prisoner so he could gather no more food supplies for the English camp.

These orders were to be obeyed until it was clear whether Captain Newport would return.

CHAPTER FOURTEEN

Fighting Back

"How do you know all this, Grandmother? It happened long before you were born."

To have the boy call me "grandmother" pleases me enormously. He is usually distant and formal, and uses my public name—as if he is keeping me at arm's length. In fact, Lost Owl seems to be keeping the whole world at arm's length. He doesn't quite trust anything to come out the way it should. It heartens me to see this grandchild of my long-dead brother lose himself enough in my narration to embrace it as a family epic instead of a tribal tragedy in which he has no part.

Old Woman chuckles from her pallet at his question. "We all know these things, child—those of us who are old enough to remember. These stories were told over and over again when we were children."

She is right.

After the uprising failed, and we were in hiding far in the interior, Opechancanough went over those early years again and again, as we sheltered ourselves beside the hearth in the dark winter evenings when wind and snow chilled the world outside. As a child, I did not question the frequent repetition of the arguments he had had with

93

Powhatan; but I understand now that he had become obsessed with defending the course he believed in.

Opechancanough was positive that Powhatan was wrong and that his own approach was right. If they had done away with Captain John Smith when they had him captive, they could have wiped out the feeble settlement that the English called Jamestown. Less than half of the white men were still alive, and they had little or nothing to eat. Half-starved and ill from drinking the brackish water, they could not survive a surprise attack. That would have been the end of it.

"What made Powhatan hesitate?"

Powhatan remembered the prophecy—or so Opechancanough believed. He argued over and over that if Jamestown was destroyed, the prophecy could never be fulfilled. He bemoaned Powhatan's fear of the white man's powers. He explained to the priests that the tricks John Smith performed were not magic at all—all the white men knew those secrets. The ivory compass with the needle that moved by itself was something every captain used. The block of paper on which John Smith made magic marks that talked to his companions had been used by many of the Spanish among whom Opechancanough had been held captive for so long.

"We could hardly believe that," Old Woman interjects ruefully. "None of us had ever seen such wonders as the English brought with them."

"But surely Powhatan respected Opechancanough's word?" Lost Owl argues.

Old Woman reaches out to pat his hand. "We are interrupting Cockacoeske's story. The best part of all is what comes next," she murmurs, her eyes glinting in anticipation.

Her enthusiasm is touching. I must not disappoint her.

Powhatan considered Opechancanough's reasoning carefully, mindful of his experiences among the Spanish. He
consulted with his council, then repeated his instructions
that Opechancanough was to keep John Smith out of
mischief and away from Jamestown until they knew whether
Captain Newport would return in the great canoes with
the guns that could destroy a village with a single volley.

Opechancanough was so disgusted with all the fuss that
the priests made over Smith's magic that he marched the
English officer out on a tour of the countryside, in spite of
it being the coldest moon of winter. They visited all of the
villages of our Pamunkey tribe, then crossed over to the
Mattaponi and paid a call at all of their hamlets. The chief
of Menapacunt,* the village located where the Pamunkey
and Mattoponi rivers' tributaries flowed together, took over
and marched Smith up to Rappahannoc country. The people up there wanted to look at the white prisoner to see if
he was the captain who had come up their river two or
three *c'hunks* earlier and treacherously killed their chief
and many of their braves.

Smith was not the culprit, so the cavalcade wandered
around the fringes of Potomac country, and finally retraced
its steps to Uttamussak, the second of our principal sacred
Pamunkey towns. They settled down there, and the priests
passed the long winter nights by arranging the sacred
sticks and rings of grain to foretell the future. They
performed their ritual dances until the dawn was break-
ing, in the hope that their mystic powers would strike awe
into the white man's heart.

Finally, a messenger slipped into the village, and
Opechancanough gave orders to march. He told Smith that
he was taking him to Great Powhatan, and they set off
toward the rising sun with Smith protesting that they
were headed in the wrong direction. He thought that the
chief he and Captain Newport had visited at the fall line
on Powhatan's river was the supreme chief. Opechancanough
ignored his stupidity and marched on.

---

*Now the location of West Point, Virginia.

When they reached Werowocomoco, a great assembly of warriors was massed outside of Powhatan's longhouse, solemnly watching the arrival of Opechancanough's prisoner. Smith was made to wait until Powhatan was ready to receive him, then he was ushered into the long hall. The supreme chief sat beyond the fire on a low platform covered with mats decorated with chains of pearls and piles of raccoon skins. His council members were seated on mats in rows on either side, with ranks of young women standing behind them, each adorned with a thick chain of white beads and red markings on her face.

Smith was received with the customary two great shouts of welcome, and then the *weroansqua* of Appamattuc, whom Smith had met before in her own village, offered him a clay bowl of water in which to wash his hands. Another woman gave him turkey feathers on which to dry them.

Finally, Powhatan spoke words of good will and beckoned his retainers to place trenchers of meat and cornbread before the Englishman. After they had eaten, they talked. Powhatan said politely, "I understand from Opechancanough that you claim knowledge of the movement of the sun, the moon, and the stars." But what our chief really wanted to find out was the reason the white strangers had come to our shores.

John Smith replied, "My men and I encountered our enemies, the Spaniards, and had to fight them. We were outnumbered and driven by adverse weather into the bay. The Kecoughtan received us and gave us fresh water, then sent us up your river, where the Pasbeheghs welcomed us. We were forced to stay on the Pasbehegh island to mend a leak in our pinnace; and we are waiting for our father, Admiral Newport, to return and conduct us away."

Opechancanough seethed through the long and devious discussion, because he didn't believe a word of what Smith was saying. His disgust was complete when Powhatan decided to confer on his English captive the honor of the ritual ceremony of death and rebirth, by which a stranger can be initiated into membership in the tribe.

When the mock executioners stood with clubs poised beside the braves who forced John Smith to his knees on the improvised altar, the final folly, in Opechancanough's estimation, was the designation of Powhatan's favorite daughter Matoaka—whom he called *Pocahontas,* or "little mischief"—to be Smith's sponsor in entering a new life as her brother in Powhatan's family.

The powwow held that night around the council fire, after Smith had been sent to sleep in another longhouse, was tense.

Although Opechancanough was in a rage, he kept his anger under rigid control, knowing that Powhatan had the power of life and death over all his subjects. "You have this white man completely in your control! None of his people are a threat to us. The encampment at Jamestown is too weak to retaliate. He killed three of our braves while we were capturing him. Their blood is on his hands and their families demand revenge. Why are you letting him live?"

"Captain Newport's ship is becalmed in a fog outside the capes," Powhatan answered quietly. "It will be a matter of only two or three days—when the fog lifts and the breeze freshens—before he reaches Jamestown."

"Then get rid of Smith before he comes! None of the English settlers know what has happened to him, other than the fact that he and his companions disappeared in Chickahamen country and never returned."

"He is a *weroance.* The English will not lightly accept the killing of their war chief. They will turn the big guns on their ships against our villages and destroy them."

"Villages can be rebuilt."

"But the only way we can escape their guns is to retreat. Will we better off, driven from the streams on which we depend for food and transport, and hiding in the forests, rather than negotiating with the Englishmen and trying to reach a peaceful agreement?"

Opechancanough tossed his head in contempt. "You are afraid of them."

"I have to decide what is best for my people," Powhatan

reasoned. "The goal we have been striving for has come to pass. Thirty bands—a hundred villages—look to me for leadership. I have at least two thousand braves under my command, but we have no weapons to match the English guns and knives. I must decide how best to use our strength and how to compensate for our weakness."

"That display you put on today for Captain Smith won't scare him."

"He must understand that our gods are powerful and mysterious too," Powhatan argued. "When he realizes that I am a great ruler with vast dominions in my power and strong warriors to command and that my priests are in communion with the Creator Ahone through his inter-mediator Okee, he and the English will be more careful in their dealings with us. They will consult me for permission to explore our lands and trade with our people."

"You are wasting your time," Opechancanough spat out. "I saw the Spanish treat our people like slaves—stealing their wealth, forcing them to work in the mines, driving them off their lands, and killing them when they would not obey. These Englishmen are no different."

Powhatan's face was sad. "Nevertheless, we cannot fight their guns with the weapons that we have. We must bargain for time, so we do not fall before this third invasion."

"You believe the prophecy." Opechancanough shook his head in frustration.

"I believe that the best way to combat it is to avoid open warfare while we convince the English that we too have strong power and can predict the future. We will not return Smith to Jamestown until the very day that Captain Newport arrives."

Two days later, John Smith was summoned again to the great council house. Two hundred warriors filed in after him, each painted black, led by Great Powhatan. He sat down on the mat facing his prisoner and told him that they were now friends, and that Powhatan would regard him as his own beloved son. He was an adopted member of Great Powhatan's personal family—a *weroance*. As proof of this, the neighboring territory of Capahowasic, downstream from Werowocomoco, would be his to govern.

A dozen braves were appointed to guide Smith back to Jamestown. Although it was only a day's march across the peninsula, they stopped for the night in a Pasbehegh hunting lodge while, unknown to Smith, they awaited news of the progress of the English vessel into the bay. Smith reached Jamestown the next morning; and before night fell, Captain Newport sailed up to the landing.

CHAPTER FIFTEEN

Fruitless Negotiations

"Was Captain John Smith really so important?" Lost Owl is tracing the pattern of the woven rushes in the mat on which he sits. As he leans over in the firelight, the sharp planes of his jaw and the arch of his neck are outlined against the shadows behind him. His skin is smooth and taut and his limbs firm and muscular with the vigor of youth, and in that moment when I am aware of his growing strength and vitality, I feel a fleeting sense of anguish that the promise of our children may never be fulfilled.

In answer to his question, I tell him that Opechancanough thought he was important—at least, he talked more of John Smith than of any other Englishman. All his life, he railed over his failure to convince Powhatan at the very beginning that outright war against the English was the only course to follow. He hated Smith for the humiliations he suffered at his hands; but the courage and determination of the stocky young English warrior in his constant struggle to keep his people alive won Powhatan's grudging admiration.

Old Woman clears her throat. "They all admired him. He was cocky and determined and not afraid of anything that walked. He understood his orders. He kept his ragged band of lazybones alive, stranded so far from their homes, in spite of their dislike of scrounging for food. They never would have survived without him."

That is true.

Lost Owl turns his attention back to me. "Then what?"

Two moons after Powhatan sent him back to Jamestown, Smith sent word that the great white chief, Captain Newport, would pay a state visit to Werowocomoco. He and Smith would have made the trip sooner, but the fort at Jamestown had burned. All the white men had been working frantically, driven by Smith during those bitter days of winter, to erect shelters for themselves and the newcomers from England.

Shortly thereafter, one of the great English canoes sailed around the peninsula and up the Pamunkey river. Smith and a half platoon of soldiers, arms readied, came ashore and marched smartly into a swamp. Powhatan sent his son Nantaquaus to rescue them and guide them to Werowocomoco. He received them in state and sat Smith in the place of honor on the mat beside him. Smith brought gifts from Captain Newport—a suit of red woolen cloth, a sugarloaf hat similar to that worn by the English king, and a tall, skinny white dog that he called a greyhound. The two spent the day matching wits, Powhatan trying to convince Smith that real friends laid down their arms.

Captain Newport came ashore the next day, preceded by a trumpeter making noises that startled the wits out of our people. After the usual pleasantries, Newport presented Powhatan with a stripling named Thomas Savage, whom he claimed was his son, as a token of good will. Not batting an eyelash, Powhatan in turn gave Newport his trusty servant Namontack to return with him to England in the place of young Savage.

Newport proved to be a far less wily negotiator than Smith. Powhatan asked him to send away his guard, which Smith always refused to do. Newport complied, and also agreed that chiefs should not haggle when they bartered.

This allowed Powhatan to set the value of the English goods brought along to exchange for food, and the value of copper pots plummeted. Smith saw what was happening, and produced some brilliantly colored Venetian beads— blue as the clear autumn sky and more beautiful than any others our people had ever seen. He priced them very high, and they won a large exchange in corn.

When the visit was concluded, Powhatan sent a gift of twenty turkeys to Newport in Jamestown, and asked for the same number of swords in return. Newport sent them, but he returned to England in the next moon, and Smith put a stop to any further exchange of arms for food.

The English weapons were so important to our people, however, that we took them whenever the opportunity arose. In exasperation, Smith threw a half dozen of our braves in jail in the fort, and sent word to all the neighboring *weroances* that all stolen tools and arms had to be returned to secure the prisoners' release. Fruitless negotiations went on for weeks, using intermediaries such as young Thomas Savage. Finally, Powhatan sent Pocahontas to Smith to swear eternal friendship and to arrange an exchange of prisoners. The wide-eyed slip of a girl, whirling on gusts of laughter into his palisade, won concessions from Smith that he had denied to stalwart braves.

Smith spent the summer exploring the rivers and our bay, and when harvest time came, Powhatan received word that Smith had been elected chief of the settlement at Jamestown. He set to immediately enlarging the fort on the island and began what he called military drills for his guard units. Our people gathered from all around the countryside to watch the English soldiers, matchlocks on their shoulders, marching stiffly up and down.

The last of the corn was being gathered when Captain Newport returned, bringing Namontack and gifts from the king in London. Smith and a handful of soldiers brought Namontack to Werowocomoco to invite Powhatan to come to Jamestown to receive the presents and a crown from King James. Powhatan was out hunting when he arrived, so Pocahontas and her friends entertained Smith with dancing and feasting while her father was summoned.

When he returned the next day, Powhatan told Smith that he was already chief of all the bands in his own country, so he had no need of a crown. If the English wanted to give him presents, they could bring them to Werowocomoco.

Smith went back to Jamestown, and he and Captain Newport returned to Werowocomoco in one of their great canoes. Newport marched ashore with his guard, wearing the full-dress regalia of the admiral of Virginia, and presented Powhatan with a silver basin and ewer, an English bed with all of its curtains and furnishings, and a scarlet cloak and other clothing appropriate to English royalty.

Powhatan permitted his shell-embroidered skin mantle to be exchanged for the English garment; but he absolutely refused to obey instructions that he must kneel to receive the copper crown.* Our chiefs show their respect for each other by exchanging highly valued copper medallions, but they never kneel to anyone—not even Okee. Smith and Newport were so adamant that they leaned on Powhatan's shoulders to demonstrate what they wanted. When Powhatan stooped slightly under the pressure, Newport slapped the crown on his head and declared him King of the Virginia Indians.

A pistol was discharged to signal the gunners on the ship, and the burst of cannon fire which followed as a salute to the newly recognized monarch badly startled Powhatan. He sprang alert, suspecting an ambush; but the English officers hastened to reassure him, while Namontack explained that this was an English custom that he had observed many times in London.

Opechancanough watched all of this with great disgust; and rightly so, he claimed, because Newport returned to England two moons later, leaving Smith in charge of two

---

*Powhatan's mantle is preserved today in the Ashmolean Museum at Oxford University in England.

hundred Englishmen. When Smith next went out to scour
the countryside for food, his attitude toward our people
was no longer friendly. Powhatan sent word to all of his
allied bands to withhold their food from the white men.

Smith went first to the Chickahamen river, where the
villagers refused to trade until Smith landed a raiding
party and threatened to burn their longhouses. Another
Englishman was sent to Werowocomoco with far less suc-
cess, although Namontack did his best to maintain amica-
ble relations. Smith set off for the Nansemond river to
collect four hundred baskets of corn that had been promised to him the previous summer. The Nansemond protested
that they had new orders from Powhatan to keep the
English out of their river. Smith again resorted to musket
fire and burning villages to get his boats loaded with
grain.

After this supply was unloaded at Jamestown, he headed
up river. The Weyanoc on both sides of the river had
disappeared completely into the forest.

Old Woman nods her approval.

The Appamattucs had only a meager supply to trade.
Other colonists who had gone hunting for food in other
directions returned empty-handed.

Knowing how desperately the English were searching
for food, Powhatan sent Namontack to Jamestown to tell
Smith that he would load his great canoe with corn if
Smith would send him men to build a house such as
Namontack had seen in London, plus a grindstone, fifty
swords, some muskets, a cock, a hen, and some copper and
beads. Smith immediately dispatched three Dutch carpen-
ters on the trail across the peninsula and set sail himself
by water. Bad weather delayed him, and our river was
frozen far out from shore when they finally arrived. The
Englishmen chopped through the ice to get the ship as
close to shore as possible; then they waded waist-deep
through the crumpled ice and oozing mud to shore.

Powhatan received them cordially, but indicated that

there was no point in their coming if they had not sent the requested swords and guns. Smith protested that there was no need for swords and guns when they were friends. This led to a long wrangle about the English going armed into our villages and taking food by force. Powhatan made it clear that he considered Smith his subject, and he should conduct himself as such.

Smith then accused Powhatan of having done away with the missing Roanoke settlers, and the two men had an argument.

Lost Owl's black eyes glitter in the firelight. "How did Smith know?"

Powhatan never found out how Smith knew about the Roanoke settlers. That was forbidden information. Apparently after Newport's visit and the business with the copper crown, someone had informed Smith of the fate that met the Roanoke settlers.

Smith was angry, and he threatened Powhatan.

The great chief answered, "What will you gain by taking by force that which you may quietly have with love? Or by destroying those who provide you with food? What can you achieve by war, when we can hide all of our provisions and flee into the forest, leaving you to starve because you have wronged us—your friends?"

The argument went on, and finally Powhatan rose, and drew his skin cape around him as if he was chilled. He told Smith that he would see to the food he demanded. Leaving two or three of his wives to entertain Smith, he pushed aside the mat covering the door and went out.

Moments later, as shadowy figures slipped silently into the area around the council house, the English soldiers standing guard sensed that something was amiss. They shouted to Smith, who came bursting out with pistols cocked, barking orders to his soldiers to prepare to fire.

Our people stood frozen in dismay as Smith ordered them to load his ship with corn, but the guns were convincing. It was a time-consuming task because the baskets of corn had to be lugged through the slush and half-frozen mud before they could be heaved onto the landing barge for transfer to the ship. By the time the job was finished, the tide had gone out and the ship was stranded on the mud flat.

Smith gave orders for the longhouse to be warmed, food provided, and Powhatan summoned; then he settled down to wait for the next tide.

Powhatan never came, and John Smith never saw him again. Instead, as he was dozing by the fire several hours later, Pocahontas slipped into the hut to warn him that he had angered her father and should leave Werowocomoco as quickly as possible.

"How did she dare?" Anne murmurs beside me.

"None of us knows, of course. No one was with her. She risked her life for Captain Smith, and I think she expected him to take her with him when he went."

"But he didn't." Anne's voice is sad. "She had to flee far away to the Potomac tribe and hide among them, so her father could not punish her for betraying him."

CHAPTER SIXTEEN

The Starving Time

Of all the bright figures who roamed through the shadowed landscapes of our past, Pocahontas is the one whom I would most like to understand. I suppose it is because she was a woman—the first of our women wise enough to accept the reality that the world as we had known it could never be the same after the coming of the white men.

Opechancanough absolutely refused to talk about Pocahontas, branding her a traitor every time her name came up; but there were others who remembered her and spoke of her with affection and respect. They still marveled at how this child, barely a woman, would go to Jamestown with braves bearing wild game in those early days; and she would charm the sturdy Captain Smith with her laughter and teasing. Dozens of strangely garbed men gathered around and shouted quips in a language she did not understand, but they could not shake her poise or inhibit the curiosity that drove her to learn all she could of their exotic ways.

On those brief excursions, she learned the English names for all of their possessions—houses, food, clothes, tools, weapons—and harsh words like fowl, biscuit, toddy, harquebus, halberd, and pike. She absorbed their language like our cornbread absorbs water, and she was soon more adept at carrying messages back and forth between her father and the English captain than any of our braves.

When I was a girl, just coming into womanhood myself, her facility in dealing with the white men seemed to me to be a remarkable achievement, and I foolishly tried to get Opechancanough to admit that Pocahontas must have been extraordinarily clever. His eyes would flash with anger when I brought up her name, and the veins in his temples would stand out.

"No sooner had her treachery warned Smith that he would have trouble with Powhatan, than Smith sailed his ship upstream to my village and demanded that I supply him with food." Opechancanough burned with rage every time he remembered how Smith got what he wanted.

While they were negotiating inside, Opechancanough's braves were stealthily surrounding the council house. One of the English soldiers dashed in to warn Smith. Without a moment's hesitation, he seized Opechancanough by the forelock that hung down over his left shoulder, stuck a pistol in his ribs, and shoved him roughly through the door. To the horror of the assembled braves, he threatened to shoot their chief on the spot unless they immediately loaded the ship standing at the riverside. After a moment of paralyzed silence, the ranks broke and the braves set to work as Smith commanded.

Opechancanough never forgave that humiliation. He knew that Smith used the same tactics of fiery anger and threats to obtain what little grain he could find in the other villages that he scoured on his way back to Jamestown. The arrogance of the English reminded him of the cruelty he had seen people with his own dark skin suffer at Spanish hands so many years before.

After Pocahontas' warning to John Smith, the hungry moons slipped slowly into spring, and the silvery gray woodlands took on a pinkish sheen as new buds freshened the oaks and beeches. When the ground was warmed, the English put two of their prisoners at Jamestown to work clearing land under the watch of an armed guard—the only way our people could be forced to toil in the fields of the white men. The land was for gardens to supply the English storehouses in the coming season.

One day, disaster was discovered in those storehouses. The grain that Smith had stolen from our villages to sustain the Englishmen was found to be half rotten and mildewed in the dampness of the cold season. What was still edible was rapidly being devoured by insects and rats—rats that had come from England with the settlers on their ships. There had been none in our country before their arrival.

The intrepid John Smith was not defeated. He sent half of his men downriver to live on oysters. Twenty were ordered to the tip of the peninsula to fish, and a similar number were dispatched upriver to the falls for the same purpose. The shad and herring were running in the river because it was the time of the blooming of the shad-flower bushes in the forest. Sturgeon were easily caught, and there were plenty of edible *tuckahoe* roots in the marshes for anyone willing to dig them. We always survived through the lean seasons by gathering wild food and game. We knew that corn could not be kept from harvest to harvest unless it was hung in the smoke over the cooking fires.

The Englishmen grumbled and procrastinated, and it was only the sheer force of Smith's will that drove them to scramble for food to sustain themselves through the moons of the planting season, until more ships arrived with supplies.

When those ships sailed away again, our sentinels discovered that Smith was gone. Some said that he was dead of a wound received when his powder bag was ignited by a careless spark; others said that he had sailed away in one of the English ships.

There was a new chief named Percy in the settlement who sent Captain Ratcliffe to Powhatan to seek more food. Ratcliffe had none of Smith's prudence and caution. Powhatan very easily put him and his whole company off guard, and Opechancanough glowed with satisfaction at this opportunity to avenge Smith's humiliating treatment. The thirty Englishmen were cut down as they relaxed at dinner. Only one managed to reach the safety of the pinnace anchored in the river.

In desperation, Percy sent another group to the Potomac tribe seeking food. They managed to collect a quantity of grain, cutting off the heads of two Potomac braves in the process. As they returned around the tip of the peninsula in their pinnace, the captain in charge of the fort there shouted over the water for them to hurry because Jamestown was starving. The men on the pinnace promptly hoisted all their sails and whipped out of the bay into the open ocean—bound for England.

Famine stalked the grim survivors in Jamestown while our chiefs argued around Powhatan's council fire over whether to wipe them out.

Our lookouts reported that the white men ate their horses, their chickens, and their cattle. Our people took care of the hogs that they had put on an island across the river. Then, the wretched settlers resorted to eating dogs, cats, rats, and mice. We heard rumors that they ate the corpses of their dead. They searched the woods for snakes and roots; and if they were not wary, they fell before our ever-vigilant sentinels.

In spite of the teeming fish in the river and the great flocks of fowl returning from the south, the surviving white men at Jamestown dwindled to no more than sixty out of the five hundred who had come from England. Opechancanough railed vainly that it was the time to strike.

Still Powhatan waited.

The first shoots of a new crop of corn and beans were greening our gardens when more great canoes arrived. There was great activity in Jamestown for the better part of a moon; then our sentinels saw the four English vessels hoist their sails and drift downstream. When they investigated, they found the settlement deserted. Runners swiftly traversed the forest paths, and soon there was great rejoicing up and down the length of our rivers.

"You see?" Powhatan taunted Opechancanough. "I knew if we were patient long enough, they would depart for good."

The fleet had barely left Powhatan's river when the rejoicing turned into bitter disappointment. While crossing the bay, they met another great fleet sailing in between the capes, bringing abundant provisions and reinforcements. Within hours, Jamestown was again swarming with activity.*

---

*Lord De La Warr's fleet arrived in 1610, just in time to save Jamestown.

CHAPTER SEVENTEEN

Treason or Tragedy?

None of my mothers or fathers ever spoke well of the time that followed. It was a period of continued harassment, frequent struggle, and further invasion of our tribal lands. In the discussions around the evening fires, Opechancanough hewed stubbornly to a single argument. "We waited too long. We could have wiped out Jamestown, but now it is too late."

"Wiping out that handful of survivors would not have prevented Lord De La Warr from coming with his great fleet," someone would remind him. Then Opechancanough would retreat into brooding silence while the others complained about the relentless friction between the English settlers and our people.

The ambushes that picked off the white men when they wandered beyond the fort's defenses were always followed by reprisals. Against Powhatan's orders, some of our people were unable to resist the temptation to slip into the fort to trade for enticing trinkets. They rationalized their greed by spying and cheating whenever the opportunity arose. Under the cover of darkness, sailors from the fleet sneaked outside the palisade at night and bartered their odds and ends for the fine animal pelts that fetched such good prices in London.

A longboat belonging to the English fort at the end of

the peninsula slipped its mooring and blew across the river. A sailor was sent over to the Warraskoyac to retrieve it, but he never returned. The English in the fort marshalled their forces, marched down to the Kecoughtan village and attacked it, driving all of our people into the forest.

When Lord De La Warr was informed, he sent an ultimatum to Powhatan. All English weapons, tools, and the like were to be returned to Jamestown, and Powhatan's subjects were to refrain from all hostile acts. Otherwise, the governor would be compelled to go to war.

Powhatan replied that the English should confine themselves to Jamestown Island—the only place they had received permission to camp. Otherwise, the chief's orders to his people were to eliminate the white men whenever they could.

The governor's response was to raid the Pasbehegh villages, burn their longhouses, and cut their corn. Even worse, the *weroansqua* and her children were seized, thrown into the river, and used for target practice. The Pasbehegh chief, Wowinchopunk himself, was killed in a subsequent skirmish.

The ambushes and harassments continued, followed by punitive raids and atrocities.

Lord De La Warr fell ill and returned to England, and his successor, Sir Thomas Dale, immediately began strengthening forts and stepping up military discipline. Women were brought from England to make homes for the white men, and two hundred artisans were brought to build houses and fortifications and pursue crafts.

Worse yet, each settler was given his own plot of land to till, broadening the acreage over which the colony spread. Worst of all, a young colonist named John Rolfe experimented with our tobacco plants until he found the best strains of leaf and way of curing it for shipment to England. The sacred weed that we smoked in our ceremonies soon became the focus of the settlers' efforts. Its cultivation required no great skill, but it required space. Our people watched the tobacco fields creep like a slow tide across our hunting grounds.

Governor Dale soon erected more forts in Kecoughtan, Chiskiak, and Arrahattoc country; then he began the establishment of a permanent town—a watch house, church, storehouse, and dwellings, all within a stout palisade—at the fall line where Powhatan's original village had been.

The moons waxed and waned, the seasons brought planting and harvest, and our people were pushed farther and farther away from the waterfronts.

One day, a message came to Great Powhatan from Captain Argall, who had replaced Captain Newport as admiral of Virginia. He had taken Pocahontas prisoner.*

The deeply-etched lines on Powhatan's face tightened in surprise. "How could he? She is among our Potomac friends and allies, married to a brave in the band of Chief Japazaws."

"Captain Argall was trading up the Potomac river, and discovered her there among Japazaws' people. He bribed Japazaws with a copper kettle to bring her on board the ship; then he sailed off with her."

Powhatan sighed. "What does Argall want?" he asked the messenger.

"He sends word that she will be released as soon as you return all English prisoners and weapons that are in your possession to Jamestown."

"We have no English prisoners—only deserters, who have come to us of their own accord seeking fellowship and freedom. Some of the settlers chafe under the harsh rules and regulations of the English governor.

"The governor wants them back, with all the weapons that we have acquired."

"We can return the Englishmen—they are no use to us—but we cannot return the weapons. We are helpless with only bows and arrows."

---

*1613.

"That may not satisfy him."

"I will offer corn—the English are always hungry. Tell Captain Argall to sail his great canoe to Werowocomoco and it will be filled with corn in return for the release of my daughter."

Argall sailed back to Jamestown, and Powhatan sent seven English deserters down to the colony. The governor held out for the return of English weapons. Powhatan sent down seven broken muskets, which our people did not know how to repair, but he was not pleased. Pocahontas was put in the charge of an English priest, who was to teach her to read and write.

The harvest season passed, and the cold winds of winter were blowing when Captain Argall and Governor Dale finally sailed up the Pamunkey river, bringing Pocahontas with them, to attempt an exchange. They anchored off of Werowocomoco, and waited for our people to come and ask them what they wanted. Word of their mission was dispatched to Powhatan, and he sent a message back that they should deal with Opechancanough, who was nearby. Dale refused, and he threatened to burn every village he could find unless his terms were met.

He went ashore to wait, taking Pocahontas with him. She stepped away from the party of Englishmen and moved toward her own people, who watched her warily. None of them had seen her since the night four *c'hunks* earlier when she had warned Captain Smith of her father's wrath.

"If my father loved me," she announced, "he would not bargain my value in old swords and guns and axes. If I am to be bartered for, I would rather dwell with the English, who truly love me."

Powhatan listened to the report of her words with narrowed eyes. "Was she speaking of her own free will, or at the bidding of the white men?"

"She came voluntarily to talk to us, and I heard no one instruct her on what to say," the messenger responded.

"She actually said that the English loved her?"

"Those were her very words—spoken coldly and haughtily. I have no doubt that she meant what she said. She gave no hint of longing to return to our forests with us." The messenger was obviously offended by Pocahontas' disdain.

Powhatan walked far on the empty trail that afternoon. The next morning, he instructed the messenger to return to Governor Dale. "Tell the governor that before the moon is full, we will send the guns, swords, and tools that he demands back to Jamestown, along with a supply of corn. We also promise to return any runaway Englishmen who come among us."

"Yes, Great Powhatan, I understand. What about your daughter Matoaka—your beloved Pocahontas?"

"Tell him that my dearest daughter Matoaka is to remain with him and be his child. She is to stay with him always, so our people can be friends."

The messenger stared at Powhatan as if he was not sure that he had heard him correctly.

"Tell Governor Dale that my allies along the lengths of the three rivers are to be included in this pledge of peace and friendship."

"All of your subjects are going to abide by this agreement?" The skepticism in the messenger's voice was obvious.

"If any of my tributaries steal from the white men, or kill their livestock, or offend them in other ways which we have forbidden, I will send them to Jamestown, where the English can punish them as they see fit."

The messenger's mouth hung open in disbelief.

Powhatan motioned him away. "Be gone, and repeat carefully what I have said."

Dale accepted Powhatan's terms and returned to Jamestown. A few days later, the arms and tools were brought to the fort there, along with the promised baskets of corn.

Barely three moons later, Pocahontas accepted the Christian name Rebecca and married John Rolfe in the church at Jamestown. She sent a message to her father, asking him to attend, but he sent his brother Opachisco and two of his sons to represent him.*

---

*1614.

CHAPTER EIGHTEEN

The Peace of Pocahontas

"According to my mother, Pocahontas' marriage came two migrations of the geese after I was born."

"Do you remember her at all?" Anne asks.

"How could I? She lived on John Rolfe's plantation—land near Henrico that Great Powhatan presented to his daughter on the occasion of her marriage. John Rolfe named it Varina for the top-grade tobacco leaf he had developed. She never came back to our village. Three *c'hunks* later, she was dead."

"Then you never saw her," Lost Owl accuses me.

"I did," Old Woman interjects. "Varina was not very far from where I grew up."

"Oh, tell us." Anne's eyes are eager.

Old Woman raises herself painfully onto one elbow to gaze into the flickering embers on the hearth. "When I was a very small girl, some of us used to paddle across the river to call at her back door. Her sister Matachanna always came out to exchange news with us. Often, Pocahontas herself would come from the front rooms and sit on the doorstep among us."

"What did she look like?"

Old Woman looks at me for a moment before she an-

swers. "She looked just like Matachanna, except that Pocahontas was much younger, wore English clothes and shoes, and bound her long hair up on the back of her head."

"I remember Matachanna," Anne murmurs. "Just barely."

"Of course. She came back to us after Pocahontas died. Matachanna was one of Powhatan's many daughters."

After her marriage, Pocahontas was soon with child. She sent an urgent request to Powhatan to let her beloved older sister, who looked after her when she was small, come to help her with the baby. It was a request he could not refuse, and Matachanna became a member of the Rolfe household.

A year after the baby Thomas Rolfe was born, the Virginia Company sent the Rolfe family to England. Matachanna went with them, as did her husband, Uttamatamakin, whom Powhatan sent as his personal emissary to King James. A dozen of our people went as well, to provide support and service to Pocahontas.

As a small child, I sat on Matachanna's knee, listening to her tales of those moons in London—the houses built so close together that no sunlight came between them; the endless streets, crowded with throngs of people; the horses and carriages that crowded people out of the way; the palaces, brilliant with golden decorations and masses of candlelight reflecting on the bright clothes of the courtiers; and the masques and balls to which Pocahontas was invited. She wore the beautiful gowns and jewels of royalty and was treated like a princess. She hoped that it would never end.

While the Rolfes were in England, the growing season faded into harvest, and the forest foliage reflected splashes of color along the riverbanks. Sunsets edged slowly along the horizon, streaking the clouds with banks of fire as the clear cold of winter crept over Powhatan's land. He was growing old and tired, and the responsibilities of his federation seemed to weigh more heavily on his shoulders than before.. As another time of rebirth finally approached, he put his brother, Opitchipan, in charge and went off to visit his allied chiefs in Potomac country.

Finally, the ship returned from England with John Rolfe and Matachanna and Uttamatamakin, but not Pocahontas. She had fallen desperately ill as they were departing, and the ship had to put back into port so she could be taken ashore and cared for. But it was too late—they buried her beside a church on the shores of England.* Her son Thomas was left in the care of an English uncle.

Uttamatamakin, who had been ordered by Powhatan to verify whether the English were as numerous as Captain John Smith had claimed, was morose. One can easily count two thousand braves on a stick no longer than the width of a man's hand by making a single notch for each time one has counted the number of one's fingers and toes, and lining the notches in rows of ten around the circumference of the stick. This is easy to do among our people, because our villages seldom have more than thirty or forty warriors. The first day that Uttamatamakin went out into the streets of London, he threw his stick away because he was so overwhelmed by the crowds of people concentrated in that one place. His report confirmed Opechancanough's prediction. The English were more numerous than the flocks of birds that laced our skies before the icy winds of winter.

Great Powhatan never reassumed his command. After receiving word of Pocahontas' death, he seemed to lose interest in the affairs of the alliance. He watched one more migration of the geese with moody, grey-filmed eyes, and he paced his beloved forests through one more sunlit spring. Then he called his tributary chiefs together in council and designated his brother, Opitchipan, to succeed him.

Soon after, runners brought us word of his death.** His women blackened their faces with soot and oil, and took

---

* At Graves End in 1617.
**1618.

turns singing the mourning chants. They cleaned his bones and filled the body cavities with shell and copper beads. The skeleton was wrapped in the softest, whitest deerskins, then laid ceremoniously to rest in the place of honor on the high rack behind the statue of Okee in the temple at Orapaks, where priests kept vigil every hour of the day and night, every day of the year.

The new Powhatan worried, temporized, and wrung his hands as the English carved vast tobacco plantations out of our wilderness. Opechancanough sat, strangely silent, through the long, inconclusive council sessions. His brooding hawk eyes were on Opitchipan, making him more nervous and uncertain than ever.

Finally, Opechancanough made a terse announcement to the assembled braves. "Opitchipan will do nothing but negotiate with the white men, while they go about robbing us of our birthright. I will fight them. You must choose between him and me."

When Opitchipan protested that he was Great Powhatan's chosen successor, Opechancanough stood his ground. "Let the kernels be counted."

Each chief was given a bean and a kernel of corn—the corn for Opitchipan, the beans against him. When the basket had been passed and each brave had dropped in his choice, the kernels were counted.

There were more beans than corn.

CHAPTER NINETEEN

Peace No More

Sometimes, when I remember Matachanna's gentle voice, it takes me back to my early childhood, when I drifted carefree through the brief interlude that the English called the Peace of Pocahontas. No war parties set off in the frozen dawns, no alarms sounded in our villages, no skirmishes caused the women and children to flee. There was no laying in wait behind blackberry thickets or hiding in the marsh grass or ambushes along the forest trails.

Matachanna was a part of that precious time. She had rocked Pocahontas' son to sleep in her kitchen and hung laundry to dry in the garden, while John Rolfe and his yoemen toiled peacefully in the tobacco fields that stretched beyond the hedge. Matachanna mourned quietly ever after for that time of serenity. She never accepted the decision to shatter that peace with the killing that Opechancanough unleashed after seven *c'hunks* of tranquility.

Anne stirs on the mat and Lost Owl looks puzzled. "She didn't prevent it," he challenges me.

I shake my head. How could she prevent it? She was only a woman. But she never accepted the plotting around the campfires.

She warned the men repeatedly of the power and wealth she had seen in London—the power that could destroy us all if Opechancanough's plan was executed. After we fled, in those many seasons that we spent hidden far from our rivers and the bay, whenever the subject of the uprising came up, Matachanna shook her head firmly and declared, "It wasn't necessary, and nothing good came of it."

Opechancanough fumed and ranted every time he heard her, but she refused to budge in her conviction. Her answer to all of his accusations was always the same. "Powhatan decided that we must live in peace with the English. He knew they were too strong for us to overwhelm them."

"They were only a handful at the end of that first winter!"

"Ah, you might have succeeded then, but no good came from attacking them so many years later."

Sometimes, Opechancanough was goaded to fury by her steady calm and shouted, "I wasn't born to do good!"

"Then why were you born?" she asked him.

"To protect my people!"

One could not doubt his conviction. Matachanna would look quietly around the small cluster of longhouses and at the tiny stream beside them that was not deep enough to float a log canoe. She would say nothing—but no one could misunderstand her meaning. Even Opechancanough could not deny our pitiful existence, and he would stride angrily away into the forest—away from the challenge in Matachanna's steady eyes.

As I grew from childhood to womanhood, I often sat beside her, helping her arrange strips of venison on the drying racks. We would yearn together for the green gardens of Orapaks and the broad river where we used to swim in the golden dawns. I could shut my eyes and bring back the memory of the clouds at sunset reflected in pink and rose on the placid water. A lazy blue heron would be skimming just above the surface, winging his way home from his favorite perch in the top of a cypress tree. We recalled the shrouded mornings when the mists rose from the river like wraiths, completely obscuring the opposite shore. Matachanna would tell me about the peaceful years she had spent with her sister in John Rolfe's comfortable house. She made it clear that Pocahontas loved John Rolfe, and that she herself found him to be a gentle and admirable man—slow to anger and always fair in his judgments.

I never tired of her stories of the days before tragedy struck us, but Matachanna assured me that, in due time, the future would become more important to me than the past. She said that it is woman's nature to affirm rather than deny.

Finally, I understood her meaning. When Totopotomoy spoke for me, her promise came true. The clearing was just as small, the stream just as shallow, and our existence just as narrow—but none of it mattered when I knew that my tall brave loved me.

Lost Owl's eyes are haunted with accusation. "Why then do you want me to let Wind Sighing go without making any effort to find her and bring her back?"

I can only sigh at the anguish in his eyes, and tell him again that she must come back of her own accord and that he cannot capture her or cage her. He hunches his shoulders and wraps his arms around his knees as if he is cold. I can see him hating the fact that he is not yet far enough into manhood to simply defy us and follow his own instincts.

Anne tries to soothe him, but he will not be placated. He tips over onto his knees, springs to his feet, and before we can protest, he flings aside the mat covering the door and disappears. His mother starts to rise to follow him, but then we hear a male voice greeting him in the clearing outside. As the murmur of conversation continues, she sinks slowly back onto her knees.

"Do you think we are wrong in discouraging him from looking for the girl?" she whispers.

"What would he do if he found her? He can hardly force her to come back."

"He is so upset."

"I know, and I ache for him. I only wish she had cared enough to wait for him."

Anne shakes her head. "He is still so young, so uncertain, so untested—"

"And so desperately seeking his place in the scheme of things." I reach for another log to throw on the glowing coals. "I wish that we could see more clearly the paths we are to follow, so we could give our children clearer directions."

My own voice trails off into the shadows, and I bow my head to hide the trembling in my fingers.

The smoke from the disturbed embers swirls upward, and soon a tongue of flame spurts through the bark of the log, throwing a sudden light across us and onto the sapling framework overhead. I look up at Anne's face; her high cheekbones and dark eyebrows are etched sharply now beneath her thick black hair.

She gazes at me with great, luminous eyes and asks quietly, "Do you think Matachanna was right?"

The abrupt change in subject startles me and forces me to collect my wandering thoughts.

Was Matachanna right in believing that Powhatan understood our predicament better than Opechancanough? That our survival depended on guarding the peace? How can I answer? I have wrestled with this question through ten thousand sleepless nights, and put it aside again on as many worried mornings. All I have concluded with any certainty is that once invaders come, you cannot go back in time to before their arrival.

CHAPTER TWENTY
A Fateful Return

As we lie sleeping, a wild errant wind gusts out of the northeast, fanning a supposedly dead fire inside a green oak log that lies under the sheltering trees beside our village. The tree had been felled by wrapping the trunk in wet clay and burning away the base. The men had also been using fire to hollow out the interior of the tree trunk before shaping it into a new canoe.

Dead leaves swirl from the branches overhead into the rescusitated embers, searing into flame and being carried by the gusts into the dry grass around the longhouses. Two of our dwellings are infernos by the time the cries of terrified families rouse the rest of the sleeping village.

Fortunately, all of the occupants escape. Okee is watching over us—the two burning longhouses stand on the downwind side of the village. We are able to beat out the flames as they crackle through the tinder-dry grass toward the remaining dwellings.

When the first dim light seeps through the heavy clouds overhead, we survey our losses and decide that we have been blessed. The whole village could easily have gone up in smoke. The shivering women and children of the two displaced families are fit in where there is room, while the men begin cutting saplings for new frameworks.

They work quickly because the wind continues to rise until it roars steadily through the tops of the pines and bare oaks, swaying them in quivering arcs and chilling the hands that struggle to tie the ranks of imbedded saplings in place. Women sort through their stores to find skin covering for the frames, while others sit beside their cooking fires with fingers flying as they weave additional mats to finish the new dwellings. Even Old Woman sits hunched over a pile of rushes, forcing knuckles crippled by age and many cold seasons to shove the flat strips into their geometric patterns.

We are engrossed in this demanding task for three days—too busy to think of anything else. When I come out of my longhouse to check on the men's progress, I am glad to see Lost Owl perched on top of one of the arched frames tying deerskins into place for insulation between the mats. He is light and agile and completely absorbed in what he is doing. I think that the physical demands of this task are a good distraction for him.

Then I see my son John West ride into the village with a much smaller figure crammed into the saddle behind him, slumped against his back. He hands down the limp body of Wind Sighing; her skin is hot and dry to our touch as we receive her.

"She is sick," he mutters. "Harris doesn't want her around anymore. She is of no use to him."

We carry her into my longhouse and lay her gently on my sleeping mats. She retches violently, then moans as the spasms cease.

"Where do you hurt, child?" I ask her.

Her face contorts and her head turns from side to side. "All over," she whispers. "My head, my back, my arms, my legs . . ."

I squat on my heels and stare bleakly at the circle of anxious faces surrounding me. Lost Owl kneels across from me, watching the girl. His mouth is open, his forehead puckered, and his nose pinched. I cannot meet his eyes. I have seen this fever many times before—it is a killer. We do not get this disease in our own villages, only when we live among the white men. Our people die like flies from it.

We do what we can to make Wind Sighing comfortable. I tell the women to bathe her hot skin with cool water and to make infusions of herbs for her to drink, then I go outside to ask further questions of John West.

He is already gone.

I stand on the hard, bare earth in front of my longhouse, the wind whipping my cape and skirt and tearing at my hair, and I wonder how this unfeeling and cowardly man can be my son—my only living son and concrete contribution to the lineage of my people.

Wind Sighing grows weaker with every passing day. Soon, she is coughing up blood, and finally, she lapses into delirium. Lost Owl sits beside her in rigid silence through the days and nights, dozing sometimes, but only leaving her side to relieve himself. We do what we can to ease her pain and keep her quiet with a potion steeped from dried May apples, but the futility of it crushes my heart.

It seems strange, but the night she dies finally brings an end to the wind that has been roaring across the land since it caught the embers and burned our longhouses. After her spirit has left us, I step outside into the vast silence of the night. I look up at the black bowl of a sky that is laced with stars and I marvel at the glory that is keeping vigil over death.

CHAPTER TWENTY-ONE

Farewell, Lost Owl

Anne rushes through the door of my longhouse at dawn the next morning, her braid loosened from sleeping and a skin blanket clutched around her against the numbing cold.

"Lost Owl is gone!"

The announcement dismays me, but as I pull myself to my feet and gather my own blanket around me, I realize that it does not surprise me.

"He has taken his father's musket and stolen away while we were sleeping!"

The log fragments on the hearth are gray and dead, and there is almost no light in my longhouse. I turn over a charred chunk and hastily drop dried pine needles on the gray coals, fanning them with a wing of turkey feathers. The needles flame and catch the chips that I add. When there are tongues of fire, I stand again, staring at Anne's stricken face, searching my mind for a reply. Nothing comes to me. I feel paralyzed, as if Lost Owl's action was so inevitable that no words are appropriate.

Anne takes a step closer and raises her voice, as if she thinks that I may not have heard what she told me. "You must send a party of men to find him and bring him back immediately—before it is too late!"

I turn my head away from her insistence. My mind is suddenly flooded with that vast majesty of stars splashed across the black sky that I gazed at the night before. The creator takes our children from us, but he gives us that awesome mystery as well, so surely there must be logic in what he does.

"It is already too late, Anne," I answer her. "Nothing we can do will bring Lost Owl back until he has accomplished what he has set out to do."

"But he will be killed!" she cries. Her voice breaks and her hands flutter helplessly in front of her.

I cannot argue with her statement.

It is very doubtful that a mere stripling like Lost Owl can succeed all alone in killing the planter Harris. Even if he does surprise him by stealth and succeeds in shooting him with a musket with which he is not very familiar, there is very little possibility that he could then escape the search parties that would be sent after him. John West would know immediately who had killed the English farmer, and he would have no compunction about telling the authorities at Middle Plantation.

Where could Lost Owl hide?

Knowing the kind of retaliation that it would bring on our village, he could not come back here. No other band of our people could shelter him without risking the same kind of retribution. I try to imagine how far he would have to flee before he could find sanctuary, and I come finally to the villages of our enemies. Even if they gave him haven, his status would be that of a fugitive—expendable whenever he was found to be an inconvenience.

"If the men left immediately, they might intercept him in time," Anne urges. "They know where Harris tills his land."

"If they bring him back today, Anne, what will keep

him here tomorrow, or the next day, or the next? Will you
post a guard over him to deter him from his mission?"

She stares at me, and I sense that she is wrestling with
my question. "You are our chief, Cockacoeske. Could you
not forbid him to pursue this foolish course?"

If chiefs, by virtue of their titles, could stay the course
of events and order them to come out right, things would
be very different now. I put logs on the fire and lean
gratefully over the small island of heat. The light from
the flames is reflected across the hearth in tiny pinpoints
in Old Woman's eyes as she listens in silence.

"Anne," I tell my niece gently, "there are some things
that a man is compelled to do, in spite of what his chief
may order."

"Lost Owl is not a man!"

"He is a man in the way he felt about Wind Sighing." I
grope for the words that I am reluctant to speak. "In order
to become a man, it may be necessary for him to attempt
what he has set out to do."

She shakes her head and sits down wearily on the low
rack that is my sleeping place. The fire is burning brightly
now, and the flames reflect in the tears welling up in her
black eyes.

"Am I to let my son go needlessly to his death?" she
asks with desolation in her voice. "He is the only son I
have."

In the long silence, the spitting of the sap in the pine
bark and the crackling of the burning wood is the only
sound between us. I struggle for the answer for which she
is waiting.

"It is the nature of men to fight when they believe their
honor and principles are threatened. In standing for those
things, they are defending what they believe makes life
worth living."

Anne bows her head, and I feel her shaking it in protest
beside me. "It is all so futile."

I take a deep breath.

"We face the world differently, Anne. Each day for us is a struggle for the survival of our children. Having lost their temples and hunting grounds, our men have lost their purpose. They no longer see the trail ahead."

Anne's lifts her face; the tears spilling onto her cheeks are molten reflections of the firelight.

"Whether we see the trail or not, we all must go on so our children and our children's children will have a path to follow."

Epilogue

Of the thirty bands allied to Powhatan when the English arrived at Jamestown Island in 1607, only five survive today.

The Pamunkey were a large band of over 2,000 people at the turn of the 17th century. They lived in several villages on the neck of land between the Pamunkey and Mattaponi tributaries, which joined to become the broad river that the English named the York. The remnants of that tribe—around a hundred people—live today on a 900-acre reservation on the Pamunkey River, thirty miles east of Richmond. About 350 acres are suitable for farming; the remaining acreage is woods and swamp, which are suitable for hunting. Like the Mattaponi (who have a 125-acre reservation on the Mattaponi River), the Pamunkey farm, hunt, fish, make pottery and beadwork for their trading post, and seek employment off of the reservation. The population is kept fairly constant by the departure of young members of the tribe—perhaps as many as 450—in search of jobs, and the return of people at retirement age.

In spite of their small numbers, the Pamunkey are regarded as the most prominent tribe in Virginia today. Perhaps their stature is due to the English naming the queen of the Pamunkey as the head of all the surviving Powhatan tribes in the 1677 treaty following Bacon's rebellion.

Their neighbors, the Mattaponi are a little over one hundred in population, with perhaps another 180 living elsewhere. They form a small, intimate community, accessible to the outside world by a main highway only a mile from their tiny reservation. Several of the men commute to outside jobs. A few of them are independent loggers. They hunt and fish in season, selling their catches of shad and herring commercially during the spring runs. Every family has a garden, and the women make beadwork to sell at their trading post. The young people generally work and live in nearby Richmond and return to the reservation when they retire.

In order to survive in the 18th century, the Virginia tribes learned English and Christianity, generally losing their Algonkin language, religion, and most of their aboriginal crafts. They all speak English today, belong to Baptist churches, and usually have English names. The prominent Pamunkey clans are Allmond, Bradby, Bradley, Collins, Langston, Miles, Page, and Southward. The Mattaponi families are named Acree, Allmond, Custalow, and Langston.

What little is left of their land—after squatters, indiscriminate selling, and disputed claims reduced it to a fraction of the original grants—is still held in common by the two groups on the reservations in the unbroken tradition since 1646, when the English assigned them reservation land in perpetuity. Mobile homes are predominant, because they can be privately owned even though the land on which they sit cannot. Every fall around Thanksgiving, the Pamunkey and the Mattaponi shoot deer or wild fowl or catch fish to carry to the governor of Virginia in Richmond in order to fulfill the promise made by Chief Necotowance in 1646 to be loyal subjects of the English Crown and of the governor in Virginia.

The residents of the two reservations pay none of the state and local taxes levied on the rest of the citizens of

Virginia. Today, each reservation is governed by a chief and an elected tribal council—a custom that had been abandoned for over a century, but was revived in the 1920s. The councils assign land to farm, lease hunting areas, and settle legal disputes that involve only their own people. Disputes involving outsiders go to the county courts, and major reservation problems can be taken directly to the governor of Virginia or to his attorney general for settlement.

To the north, on the river named after them, you can still find the Rappahannock. About 750 of them have survived. Most are farmers and unskilled laborers who have had very limited educational opportunities and are all too familiar with poverty. Around one hundred Nansemond live on the south shore of the James River in the Norfolk/Portsmouth area. Five hundred Monocans, Powhatan's ancient enemies to the west of the fall line, still live in Virginia.

The Chickahominy (called Chickahamen in this book) have survived in greater numbers than the Pamunkey, Mattaponi, and Rappahannock tribes. Over one thousand Chickahominy live today on both sides of the river with the same name. Many of them own farms interspersed among whites and blacks. They are known by their reservation cousins as 'citizen' Indians, because they own their land individually and pay taxes on it, rather than sharing it communally in the ancestral tradition.

The groups are friendly, and family names are a good indication of the intermarriage that has taken place among them over the years. The prominent Chickahominy family names include Adkins, Bradby, Canady, Eagle, Holmes, Jefferson, Jones, Littlebear, Shongo, Stewart, Whitehead, and Wynn.

The Chickahominy would like all the tribes to work together, in contrast to the two reservation groups, who have been reluctant to join cooperative movements on the grounds that each tribe should look after its own affairs. The difference in their viewpoints hinges, of course, on how their interests can best be safeguarded. The Virginia tribes have struggled for three hundred years to maintain their identities, and they have waited three centuries to be recognized as equal citizens in the land of their fathers. In the interim, they were castigated as non-whites and lumped with the Africans imported to till the tobacco fields. After the uprising in 1622, the English passed a law making it legal to enslave local Native Americans. Few met that fate—they preferred death to slavery—but those who did were completely assimilated with the black population.

The 1705 Black Code established one non-white category in Virginia, thus depriving the Native Americans of their civil rights. Their situation became particularly difficult during the Civil War, when the local whites confiscated their rifles, assuming (correctly) that the Indians were hostile toward them. For people who relied on hunting for much of their food, it was a disastrous deprivation. The Pamunkey went to Virginia's governor to protest, and he agreed that the action was not legal. Both the Pamunkey and the Mattaponi withdrew from the local churches when the war ended in 1865, and they formed their own. These separate Native American churches have ever since been a major focus of tribal stability.

The Jim Crow legislation passed in the 1880s applied to the Native Americans as well as blacks, so the tribal men began to wear their hair long to identify themselves and adopted strong sanctions against intermarriage with blacks. In the following decades, there was an upsurge of Indian pride in Virginia that was sparked by James Mooney of the Smithsonian Institution. He encouraged the able Pamunkey chief, George Major Cook, to speak out against the sufferings of his people.

The Virginia Racial Integrity Law of 1924 set rigorous

definitions of white, red, and black races. Geneological data indicating any blood mixture was used to keep Indians and Negroes "in their places." Most Virginians regarded the Native Americans as blacks and treated them accordingly. Literacy tests kept many from voting—nearly all of the Rappahannock, for example, who had no school, were illiterate.

The Chickahominy started their own school in the 1920s to avoid having their children sent to all-Negro schools. They worked diligently for many years to expand it to include all twelve grades. When Virginia integrated its schools in 1966, the Chickahominy school was taken over by the state. Its integration as an elementary school ended its separate standing and required many of the Chickahominy children to be bussed to other schools—an ironic twist in the long struggle to educate their children.

Although their situation was improved by it—particularly in the expansion of their voting rights—the Virginia tribes did not participate in the civil rights movement of the 1950s and 1960s. High school courses were added to the reservation schools, and city jobs that had not been available before opened up to them. These changes, however, generated little enthusiasm for greater participation in white governmental institutions among the Native Americans. Instead, they focused their attention on their separate tribal churches and on tribal councils with elected chiefs. The Chickahominy revived the Powhatan Confederacy in 1971, but the reservation groups held back.

In 1983, the Virginia General Assembly established the Council on Indians to gather information, make studies, and conduct research on Native Americans in the state. The intent was to suggest ways in which the Virginia tribes might reach their full potential as citizens of the Commonwealth. The Council was composed of twelve members appointed by the governor, nine of whom were Native Americans. Unfortunately, the 1991 budget crunch eliminated funds for a separate state government agency to support the council.

* * * *

Cockacoeske's forests are peaceful now.

Great stretches of them remain, greening the banks of the rivers with their tall crowns and cool shade. The sticky clay soil on the high banks that was once planted with tobacco has been abandoned and allowed to grow back naturally. Today, deer run free through the silent glades and opossum, rabbits, raccoons, and squirrels frisk through the underbrush as they did in Cockacoeske's time. The American pigeons and black bears, whose meat she savored, are gone now; but wild turkeys and cheery whistling quail still raise their springtime broods.

Pink moccasin flowers and fragile Indian pipes push up through the carpets of pine needles and oak leaves, and great stretches of dogwoods flash banners of white blossoms in the spring and crimson foliage in the fall. The maycocks and persimmons still drop the juicy fruits that she gathered with such relish; and the swamps along the many feeder streams are rank with the bladderwort and arrow-alum plants that she called *tuckahoe*.

Schools of minnows riffle the shallow waters of her rivers, while the blue heron watches motionless from his favorite lookout in the top of a cypress tree. In the fall, the wavering strings of Canadian geese wing low over the rivers in the sunsets, braking to land on the sheltered backwaters to rest and feed on their migrations. Every now and then, a bald eagle or a clutch of wild swans skims low over the shores she loved so well.

Some of Cockacoeske's wilderness has, of course, been put to the plow or built into villages and towns. More of it is now being built into suburban housing developments. All of it is threaded with highways. If Cockacoeske were to come back today and stand by the marshes along the

Pamunkey and Mattaponi Rivers, she could gaze at segments of unsullied landscape and feel the presence of her ancestors. Some of the white invaders have seen the same beauty in her forests and have left them as they were when her people roamed their endless paths.

Perhaps she roams there still.

When the fragrant honeysuckle and wild grape tangle the newly greened clearings, the smell of pine needles hangs heavy in the summer heat, or the long shafts of early morning sun spear the autumn mists that shroud the tall oaks, does her spirit linger there behind the shadows? Or does she pace strange sidewalks beside the remnants of her tribe, jostling their elbows and whispering, "Remember me?"

Bibliography

Arber, Edward, and A. G. Bradley, eds. *Travels and Works of Captain John Smith, President of Virginia & Admiral of New England.* 2 vols. Edinburgh: 1910.

Axtell, James. *The European & the Indian: Essays in the Ethnohistory of Colonial North America.* New York: Oxford University Press, 1981.

————. *The Invasion Within: The Contest of Cultures in Colonial North America.* New York: Oxford University Press, 1985.

Barbour, Philip. *The Three Worlds of Captain John Smith.* Boston: 1964.

————. *Pocahontas and Her World.* Boston: 1970.

Bridenbaugh, Carl. *Jamestown 1544-1699.* New York: Oxford University Press, 1980.

Corbitt, David Leroy, ed. *Explorations, Descriptions, and Attempted Settlements in Carolina, 1584-1590.* Raleigh, North Carolina: 1948.

Holland, C. G. "How Pocahontas Said it to Her Daddy," *The Quarterly Bulletin of the Archeological Society of Virginia* 15 (1960-61): 1-3, 16 (1961-62): 1-2.

Lewis, Clifford M., and Albert J. Loomie. *The Spanish Jesuit Mission in Virginia, 1570-72.* Chapel Hill, North Carolina: 1953.

McCary, Ben C. "Indians in Seventeenth Century Virginia." *Jamestown 350th Anniversary Historical Bulletin* 18 (1957).

Mossiker, Frances. *Pocahontas.* New York: 1976.

Percy, George. "A trewe Relacyon of the Procedeinges and Occurentes of Momente wch have hapned in Virginia from 1609 untill 1612." *Tyler's Quarterly Historical and Genealogical Magazine* 3 (1922): 259-282.

Porter, Charles W., III. *Adverturers to a New World, The Roanoke Colony, 1585-87.* Washington, D.C.: 1972.

Purchas, Samuel. *Purchas, His Pilgrimage.* London: AMS Press, 1907.

————. *Purchas, His Pilgrimes.* London: AMS Press, 1907.

Quinn, David Beers. *England and the Discovery of America, 1481-1620.* New York: 1974.

————, ed. *The Roanoke Voyages 1584-1590.* Cambridge: 1955.

Stratchey, William. *The Historie of Travell into Virginia Britania.* London: 1953.

Sturtevant, William C., and Bruce G. Trigger. *Handbook of North American Indians.* Vol. 15 Northeast. Washington, D.C.: USGPO, 1978.

Virginia Company of London Staff. *The Records of the Virginia Company of London.* Edited by Susan Myra Kingsbury. 4 vols. Washington, D.C.: AMS Press, 1935.